natalie

P9-DXN-322

GREGG
SHORTHAND
DICTIONARY

By

JOHN ROBERT GREGG, S.C.D.

Anniversary Edition

GREGG PUBLISHING DIVISION
McGraw-Hill Book Company, Inc.
New York Chicago San Francisco Dallas Toronto London

GREGG SHORTHAND DICTIONARY

ANNIVERSARY EDITION

Shorthand Plates Written by
WINIFRED KENNA RICHMOND

PUBLISHED BY GREGG PUBLISHING DIVISION
McGraw-Hill Book Company, Inc.
Printed in the United States of America

PREFACE

The preparation of the Anniversary Edition of the Gregg Shorthand Manual was a big undertaking. When it was finished, there remained tasks almost as great in the revision of "Progressive Exercises," "Gregg Speed Studies," and the keys to all these books. These done, we were obliged to revise all of the supplementary books in harmony with the changes that had been made. It is with a sigh of relief that we put the finishing touches on this Dictionary, which practically completes the series.

In the revision of all the basic texts, we were not content with changing the forms for words affected by the changes in the Anniversary Edition, or with substituting new exercises in accordance with the new arrangement of the rules and material, because we wanted to give effect to many improvements suggested by our study and experience with the old editions, or which were suggested by our many teacher friends. All the books incorporate new ideas, new material, new methods.

Now as to this Dictionary: The new features are fully set forth in the Introduction—features that I believe will render the book much more valuable than any previous edition.

In sending it forth, I desire to acknowledge my indebtedness to Mr. Rupert P. SoRelle and Mr. Louis A. Leslie for their assistance in compiling the lists of words used, and in classifying them in the manner set forth in the Introduction. Special credit should be given Mrs. Winifred Kenna Richmond for the artistic manner in which she has written the shorthand forms.

JOHN ROBERT GREGG.

INTRODUCTION

A dictionary is primarily a reference book. A good dictionary, however, properly used, should be far more than that. This is particularly true of a shorthand dictionary, which should be a guide so clear that a beginner can readily locate the shorthand outline for any given word, but which at the same time should possess all the resources needed to satisfy the most advanced writer, whether a teacher or a court reporter.

The Gregg Shorthand Dictionary should not only teach the beginner, but should help the expert to crystallize his knowledge by careful classification of the shorthand forms and consistency in the use of abbreviating devices.

In the present dictionary, we have endeavored to do these things. In this brief Introduction we shall state some of the principles followed in obtaining consistency of outline. These rules cover the treatment of some frequent sound combinations, and a thorough acquaintance with them will often make it unnecessary to refer to the word list itself for an outline.

One of the most fascinating features of Gregg Shorthand is the manner in which the principle of analogy is applied. Nothing is more helpful to the shorthand writer than this principle properly used. In effect, it means that, once you have learned the forms for one or more words of any classification, you may then write any similar word ending in the same way. For example, when you know the shorthand forms for *agitate* and *hesitate,* and therefore know that the ending *tate* is expressed by *ta,* you can write any similar words, such as *dictate* or *imitate.*

In other words, the material given in this Introduction is not to be memorized, but is to be studied intelligently in order that you may see the underlying principles governing the formation of the outlines. Nothing is arbitrary —there is always a *reason why,* even though at first sight it may not be apparent.

First, we should explain that the following have been eliminated as being unnecessary:

1. Short, simple words that any student who is still working on the early part of the Manual can easily write, such words as *cat, dog,* etc.

2. Purely "dictionary words." Every word in the list of nearly 19,000 is a word in good usage. If any of the words seem unfamiliar to you, however, look them up in an ordinary English dictionary and jot down the definition in your shorthand dictionary.

3. Certain derivatives that are formed in accordance with the rules given in the textbook, such as the numerous derivatives of the suffix *ulate,* and some others. In order to save space and make room for more root words, a complete table of these suffix derivatives is given in this Introduction. In case there should be doubt as to the correct writing of one of the derivatives, reference to this table will make the matter clear.

The Gregg Shorthand Dictionary contains the following indispensable features:

1. A list of the 19,000 most frequently used words in the English language. The words for which the shorthand forms are immediately obvious have been omitted.

2. Many past tenses, plurals, and other derivative forms that were not included in previous editions of the shorthand dictionary.

3. Derivatives in every case grouped under the root word in easily accessible form. Since the root words in type project slightly beyond the margin of the type column, the finding of any word is greatly facilitated—it is necessary only to look down the comparatively small list of root words that stand out at the left of each column.

4. Direct derivatives, and in some cases closely allied words, are listed under their root words. This has been done in order to emphasize the value of the analogical building of outlines, and also in the belief that the practice of a group of related outlines is more valuable than the practice of the isolated outlines.

FOUR FREQUENTLY USED DERIVATIVES

The four derivatives most frequently formed are the past tense, the plural, the negative, and the comparative and superlative degrees of adjectives.

THE PAST TENSE. It may be helpful to summarize and condense the rules given in the Manual for the formation of the past tense.

1. After abbreviated words, a disjoined *t* is placed close to the preceding character to express the past tense. This includes:
    a. Brief forms, as in *changed*.
    b. Words written in accordance with the abbreviating principle, as in *established*.
    c. Words written with a suffix, as in *insulted*.
    d. Words in which the last letter of the primitive form is omitted, as in *demanded*.

2. A disjoined *t* is used to express the past tense after words written in full when the joining of the *t* or *d* would not give a distinctive or facile outline, as in *fancied, glared, neared*.

3. The past tense is expressed by joined *t* or *d*:
    a. After words written in full, as in *printed, checked*, except in the few cases coming under the preceding paragraph.
    b. In derivatives ending in *ct*, as in *contracted*.
    c. In verbs ending in *l*, the special method described in paragraph 136 in the Manual is used, as in *killed*.
    d. After suffixes that give a facile and legible joining, as in *mentioned, stipulated*.
    e. After many brief forms containing the last character of the word, as in *asked, charged, worked*.

PLURALS. The formation of plurals is clearly explained in paragraphs 55, 74, and 83 in the Manual.

NEGATIVE FORMS. The vowel is omitted in the prefixes *en, in, un, em, im, um* when the prefix is followed by a consonant, as in *unseen, impossible, unmask, uninvited, unimportant*.

When a vowel follows a prefix, the initial vowel is written, as in *uneasy*, unless the vowel that follows belongs to another prefix or to a brief form, in which case it is not necessary to insert the vowel in the negative prefix, as in *inexpensive, unorganized*.

Negative words beginning with *un* or *im* in which the *n* or *m* is doubled are distinguished from the positive forms by omitting one of the doubled consonants and inserting the initial vowel, as in *unknown, immodest*.

COMPARATIVE AND SUPERLATIVE FORMS. The comparative form of an adjective is usually written by simply joining an *r* to the primitive form, as in *quicker, slower.* If, however, the adjective is written in full and ends in a straight line, the reversing principle is used for the comparative form, as in *larger, later;* when a brief form ends with the last consonant of a word, the reversed circle is used to make the comparative form after straight lines, as in *sooner, stranger;* after brief forms, abbreviated words, and words ending in a reversed circle, a disjoined *r* is used, as in *worker, purer, nearer,* unless the joined form is distinctive, in which case it may be used, as in *smaller, greater.*

The termination *est* is expressed by *es* in words ending in a consonant when the word is written in full, as in *cheapest, broadest.* This rule also applies to brief forms or contractions when the final consonant of the short-hand form is also the final consonant of the word, as in *soonest, strangest.*

The termination *est* is usually expressed by a disjoined *st* after brief forms, abbreviated words, or words ending in a vowel, as in *stillest, busiest,* but the *st* may be joined when a distinctive form is obtained, as in *fullest, truest.*

FORMATION OF ADVERBS. Adverbs formed by the addition of *ly* to the adjective are written in shorthand by adding the small circle, signifying *ly,* to the primitive form of the adjective. The only exceptions to this rule are *friendly, immediately, thoroughly, respectfully.*

THE ENDING TION

So many words end with the suffix *tion,* in its various spellings, that in forming derivatives a shorthand outline is considered to end with the final letter of a word if the word ends with the suffix *tion.* By so doing, that great class of words may be written in accordance with such rules as those in par-agraphs 76 and 59 (2) of the Anniversary Manual.

Words ending in *tionist* are written with the joined *es,* as in *abolitionist, evolutionist, elocutionist.* So, also, we are able to use the reversed circle for such forms as *auctioneer, stationer, executioner,* and the joined *d* for forms like *mentioned, commissioned, old fashioned.*

Other examples showing the manner in which the outlines ending in *tion, sion, cien* may be regarded as written in full are such classes of words as *professional, national, provisional, sensational, rational; efficient, deficient, proficient; efficiency, deficiency, proficiency.*

THE ENDING ATE

T is omitted in the terminations *rate, late, tate.* The *t* is written in the terminations *fate, vate, mate, nate.* The *at* is omitted in the terminations *cate, gate.* The following brief list of examples will make this clear:

-rate   accurate, commemorate, confederate, decorate, liberate, narrate, obdurate, operate, penetrate, perpetrate, venerate, vibrate. (In a few words the abbreviating principle is applied: *coöperate, elaborate, inaugurate, recuperate, refrigerate, separate.* To form derivatives add *s* for *-rates,* a disjoined *v* for *-rative,* a disjoined *r* for *-rator.*)

-late   annihilate, desolate, dilate, disconsolate, inflate, isolate, mutilate, oscillate, scintillate, translate, violate, ventilate.

-tate   agitate, annotate, devastate, dictate, facilitate, felicitate, gravitate, hesitate, imitate, irritate, necessitate, rotate, vegetate. (Except *meditate.*)

-fate,   phosphate, aggravate, captivate, cultivate, elevate, excavate, reno-
  -vate   vate.

-mate   animate, chromate, consummate, cremate, estimate, intimate, sublimate, ultimate, primate.

-nate   alienate, alternate, assassinate, coördinate, dominate, eliminate, fascinate, illuminate, incriminate, indeterminate, inordinate, nominate, originate, predominate, subordinate, terminate, unfortunate. (In the terminations given above, the *t* is retained when a double vowel precedes, as in *affiliate, alleviate, appropriate, conciliate, create, delineate, humiliate, radiate,* except *retaliate, appreciate, enunciate.*)

-cate   abdicate, adjudicate, complicate, confiscate, delicate, deprecate, eradicate, fabricate, implicate, indicate, intricate, locate, allocate, dislocate, lubricate, medicate, suffocate, syndicate, vindicate. (Write *ksh* for *-cation* in words so abbreviated. There are special abbreviations for *certificate, duplicate, communicate, prevaricate, reciprocate, educate.* We write in full for the sake of greater legibility the words *vacate, desiccate, dedicate, predicate, extricate, advocate.*)

-gate   abrogate, aggregate, castigate, congregate, conjugate, corrugate, instigate, interrogate, investigate, irrigate, litigate, mitigate, navigate, obligate, propagate, relegate, segregate, subjugate, surrogate, variegate. (Write *gsh* for *-gation* in words so abbreviated. The abbreviating principle is applied to *delegate, promulgate.* We write in full *legate, frigate.*)

MODIFICATION OF WORD FORMS

In forming compound words, it is often necessary to change somewhat the form of one of the words. Examples of this are: *cobweb, featherweight, flywheel, footwear, neckwear, hoodwink, horsewhip, lukewarm, milkweed, whirlwind.*

FREQUENTLY RECURRING SYLLABLES

The principle of analogy is of the greatest value to the writer of a system in which it may be used to its fullest extent, as is the case with Gregg Shorthand. We shall point out here some of the useful analogical forms that are not given as such in the Manual; many of them fall under the abbreviating principle. In order to conserve space, the shorthand forms are not given, as they may easily be ascertained from the word list of this dictionary. Knowing the outline for any one of the words, and knowing that all similar combinations are written analogically, it will be a simple matter to construct the outlines for yourself. The lists are given for convenience in practice and so that you may study the application of the principle:

-ish   abolish, banish, blemish, brutish, burnish, cherish, childish, famish, finish, flourish, foolish, furnish, girlish, nourish, perish, polish, punish, relish, Spanish, stylish, tarnish, vanish, varnish.

-let   booklet, bracelet, circlet, coverlet, eyelet, gauntlet, gimlet, goblet, inlet, outlet, ringlet, streamlet, tablet, violet. (The ending *ette* is written in full, as in *palette, roulette, silhouette.*)

-cious   (All but a few words with this ending may be written under the abbreviating principle without the *us.*) audacious, atrocious, avaricious, capacious, delicious, efficacious, facetious, fallacious, ferocious, fictitious, loquacious, malicious, meretricious, ostentatious, pernicious, precocious, propitious, sagacious, spacious, superstitious, tenacious, veracious, vivacious, voracious. (In some words having the *cious* ending, it is advisable to add the *us* in order to secure a more legible outline. This is usually true of words having a similar form in *tion,* as in *captious, cautious, infectious, suspicious, vexatious, vicious.*)

-fuse   confuse, diffuse, infuse, profuse, refuse, transfuse.

-nction compunction, conjunction, disjunction, function, injunction, junction, sanction.

-mand   command, countermand, demand, reprimand.

-ive   arrive, deprive, derive, revive, survive.

-meter   barometer, chronometer, speedometer, thermometer, diameter.

-pel   compel, dispel, expel, impel, propel, repel, spell. (The past tense of all the words ending in *pel* is formed by raising the end of the *l* to show the addition of *d*. Most of them form a derivative in *pulsion*, which is indicated by the addition of *tion* to the primitive form.)

-volve   devolve, evolve, involve, revolve. (Cf. *absolve, dissolve, resolve.*)

-tain   attain, ascertain, captain, certain, contain, detain, entertain, fountain, maintain, mountain, obtain, pertain, sustain.

-uate   accentuate, actuate, attenuate, effectuate, extenuate, graduate, insinuate, perpetuate. (All these words form derivatives in *tion*.)

-ject   abject, deject, eject, inject, project, reject.

-tern,   cistern, eastern, lantern, modern, nocturne, pattern, subaltern,
-dern   western.

-gent,   contingent, diligent, divergent, emergent, exigent, indigent, indul-
-gence   gent, intelligent, negligent. (All these words form a derivative in *gence,* and some in *gency.*)

-port   comport, deport, disport, export, import, passport, purport, sport.

-verse,   diverse, diversity, diversion, diverge; converse, conversion, con-
-versity,   verge; perverse, perversity, perversion; adverse, adversity; inverse,
*-version,*inversion; reverse, reversion; subversion; obverse; university. (*Uni-*
-verge   *verse* is written under the abbreviating principle.)

-titude   altitude, aptitude, certitude, fortitude, latitude, platitude. (Except *gratitude.*)

-ric   bishopric, cambric, choleric, fabric, gastric, lyric, metric, theatric.

-vity   brevity, levity, nativity, passivity, captivity, activity, gravity, productivity.

-ntic   romantic, pedantic, Atlantic, authentic.

-ngle   angle, bangle, bungle, entangle, disentangle, mingle, mangle, surcingle, tangle, tingle, wrangle. (The *l* is omitted from the word *single* as the word occurs so frequently. The *l* is also omitted from such derivatives of *angle* as *rectangle, triangle, quadrangle.*)

-ular   angular, cellular, jugular, muscular, nebular, ocular, oracular, secular, tabular, titular, tubular, vehicular. (We may take advantage of the abbreviating principle, however, in *binocular, molecular, spectacular, vernacular; singular, rectangular, triangular.*)

-arious   gregarious, multifarious, nefarious, precarious, vicarious.

-uous   arduous, assiduous, contemptuous, continuous, deciduous, fatuous,

incongruous, ingenuous, impetuous, presumptuous, sinuous, stren-
uous, sumptuous, tempestuous, tortuous, unctuous, virtuous.

-eous beauteous, bounteous, courteous, cutaneous, duteous, erroneous,
extraneous, hideous, igneous, piteous, plenteous.

-tial, artificial, beneficial, circumstantial, commercial, credential, essen-
-cial tial, influential, initial, judicial, martial, partial, penitential, pestilen-
tial, providential, provincial, prudential, residential, social, sub-
stantial, superficial.

DERIVATIVES OF COMMON ENDINGS

In the following list of the derivative forms of the suffixes and common
endings of words, one complete set of derivatives is given in each case. From
the outlines on the next page, any similar words may be constructed:

-scribe describe, describes, described, description, descriptive, describable,
subscriber.

-pose dispose, disposes, disposed, disposition, disposable.

-pute dispute, disputes, disputed, disputation, disputable, disputant.

-spect prospect, prospects, prospected, inspection, prospective, prospector.

-quire acquire, acquires, acquired, acquisition, acquirement.

-pire aspire, aspires, aspired, aspiration, aspirant.

-city capacity, capacities.

-sure measure, measures, measured, measurable, measurement, measure-
less.

-flect reflect, reflects, reflected, reflection, reflective, reflector.

-sult consult, consults, consulted, consultation, consultative, consultant.

-tic critic, critics, critical, critically.

-ulate emulate, emulates, emulated, emulation, emulative, emulator, emu-
latory, postulant, immaculately.

-logy psychology, psychologic, psychological, psychologically, psycholo-
gist, psychologists, psychologize, theologian.

-ograph photograph, photographs, photographed, photography, photogra-
pher, photographic, photographical, photographically.

-egraph telegraph, telegraphs, telegraphed, telegraphy, telegrapher, tele-
graphical, telegraphically.

-stic domestic, domestics, domesticate, domesticates, domesticated, do-
mestication, domestically.

DERIVATIVES OF COMMON ENDINGS

-scribe

-pose

-pute

-spect

-quire

-pire   -city

-sure

-flect

-sult

-tic   -ulate

-logy

-ograph

-egraph

-stic

GREGG SHORTHAND DICTIONARY

A

aback
abaft
abandon
abandonment
abate
abatable
abated
abatement
unabated
abbot
abbreviate
abbreviation
unabbreviated
abdicate
abdicated
abdication
abdomen
abdominal
abduct

abduction
abed
aberrance
aberrant
aberration
abet
abeyance
abhor
abhorrence
abhorrent
abide
abjure
abjuration
abjures
ablative
able
ability
able-bodied
ably
disability

disable
enable
inability
unable
ablution
abnegation
abnormal
abnormality
abnormity
aboard
abolish
abolition
abolitionist
abominate
abominable
abomination
aboriginal
aborigines
abound
about

whereabouts	absolute	abuses
above	absolutely	abusive
abrade	absolution	disabuse
abrasion	absolutism	abut
abrasive	absolve	abutment
unabraded	absorb	abutter
abreast	absorbed	abyss
abridge	absorbent	abysmal
abridgment	absorption	acacia
unabridged	abstain	academy
abrogate	abstainer	academic
abrogated	abstemious	academician
abrogation	abstinence	accede
abrupt	abstinent	accelerate
abruptly	abstract	acceleration
abruptness	abstractedly	accelerator
abscess	abstraction	accent
abscond	abstruse	accentuate
absconder	absurd	accentuation
absence	absurdity	unaccented
absent	abundance	accept
absentee	abundant	acceptability
absently	superabundant	acceptable
absent-mindedly	abuse	acceptance
absinth	abused	acceptation

accepts	unaccompanied	inaccurately
non-acceptance	accomplice	accuse
unacceptable	complicity	accusation
access	accomplish	accusative
accessibility	accomplishment	accustom
accessible	accord	unaccustomed
accession	accordance	acerbity
accessory	accordingly	acetate
inaccessible	accordion	acetic
accidence	accost	acetylene
accident	accosted	achievement
accidental	account	achromatic
accidents	accountable	acid
acclaim	accountancy	acidity
acclaimed	accountant	acidulate
acclamation	unaccountable	acidulous
acclimate	accredit	acknowledge
acclimatize	accretion	acknowledges
accolade	accrue	acknowledgment
accommodate	accrual	acolyte
accommodation	accumulate	aconite
unaccommodating	accurate	acorn
accompany	accuracy	acoustic
accompaniment	accurately	acquaint
accompanist	inaccuracy	acquaintance

acquaintances	active	adamantine
unacquainted	activity	adapt
acquiesce	actor	adaptability
acquiescence	actress	adaptable
acquiescent	acts	adaptation
acquire	enact	adapter
acquired	inactive	adaptive
acquirement	inactivity	addendum
acquires	react	addenda
acquisition	reactionary	adder
acquisitive	reenact	addict
acquittal	transact	addiction
acrid	actual	addition
acridity	actuality	additional
acrimonious	actually	additionally
acrimony	actuary	address
acrobat	actuate	addresses
acrobatic	actuated	addressograph
acropolis	acute	readdressed
across	acuity	self-addressed
acrostic	acumen	unaddressed
act	acuteness	adduce
acted	adage	adduces
action	adagio	adenoid
actionable	adamant	adept

adequate	adjust	admixture
adequacy	adjustable	admonish
adequately	adjuster	admonition
inadequate	readjust	admonitory
adhere	unadjusted	adobe
adhered	adjutant	adolescence
adherence	administer	adolescent
adherent	administration	adopt
adheres	administrative	adoption
adhesion	administrator	adoptive
adhesive	administratrix	adore
adieu	admirable	adorable
adjacent	admiral	adoration
adjective	admiralty	adorn
adjoin	admiration	adornment
adjoined	admire	unadorned
adjourn	admirer	adroit
adjourned	admires	adsorption
adjudge	admissible	adulation
adjudicate	admissibility	adult
adjudication	admission	adulterate
adjudicator	inadmissible	adulteration
adjunct	admit	unadulterated
adjure	admittance	adumbration
adjures	admitted	ad valorem

advance
advanced
advancement
advances
advantage
advantageous
advantages
disadvantage
advent
adventitious
adventure
adventurer
adventuresome
adventurous
adverb
adverbial
adverse
adversary
adversity
advert
advertise
advertisement
advertiser
advice
advisability

advisable
advised
adviser
advises
advisory
inadvisable
advocate
advocacy
adz
Aeolian
aeon
aerate
aerial
aerify
aesthetic
aesthetics
affable
affability
affect
affectation
affectionate
disaffected
unaffectedly
affiance
affidavit

affiliate
affiliated
affiliation
affinity
affirm
affirmation
affirmative
disaffirm
affix
afflatus
afflict
affliction
affluence
afford
afforded
affright
affront
effrontery
aforementioned
aforesaid
afraid
unafraid
after
afterclap
after-dinner

aftermath	agile	air-tight
afternoon	agility	airway
afterthought	agitate	alabaster
afterwards	agitated	alacrity
again	agitation	alarm
against	agitator	albatross
ageless	agnostic	albino
agent	agnosticism	album
agency	agony	albumen
reagent	agonize	alchemist
agglomeration	agrarian	alcohol
agglutination	agree	alcoholic
aggrandize	agreeability	alcoholism
aggrandizement	agreeable	non-alcoholic
aggravate	agreed	alcove
aggravated	agreement	alderman
aggravation	disagreeable	alert
aggregate	agriculture	algebra
aggregation	agricultural	algebraic
aggress	agronomy	alibi
aggression	aground	alien
aggressive	ague	alienable
aggressor	ailanthus	alienate
aggrieved	aileron	alienist
aghast	airily	inalienable

alike	allure	altogether
alimentary	alluvial	altruism
alimony	almanac	altruistic
aliquot	almighty	alum
alive	almond	aluminum
alkali	almost	alumnus
alkaline	alms	alumni
alkaloid	aloud	always
allegation	alphabet	amalgam
allegiance	alphabetic	amalgamate
alleviate	alphabetical	amalgamation
alleviation	already	amanuensis
alliance	also	amaranth
alligator	altar	amateur
alliteration	alter	amatory
allocate	alterable	amazed
allocution	alteration	amazement
allopathy	unalterable	ambassador
allotment	altercation	ambassadorial
allow	alternate	amber
allowable	alternation	ambidextrous
allowance	alternative	ambient
disallow	alternator	ambiguous
allude	although	ambiguity
allusion	altitude	ambition

ambitious	amnesty	anagram
amble	among	analogy
ambrosia	amongst	analogous
ambrosial	amorous	analyze
ambulance	amortize	analysis
ambuscade	amortization	analyst
ambush	amount	analytical
ameliorate	amounted	angel
amelioration	amperage	angelic
amenable	amphibious	archangel
amend	amphibian	anger
amendment	ample	angrily
amenity	amplification	angle
American	amplifier	quadrangle
un-American	amplitude	rectangle
amethyst	amputate	triangle
amiable	amputation	Anglo-Saxon
amiability	amuse	anguish
amicable	amuses	angular
amity	anachronism	angularity
unamiable	anachronistic	aniline
amidships	anaconda	animadversion
ammonia	anaemia	animal
ammunition	anaesthesia	animate
amnesia	anaesthetic	animated

animation	annoyance	antagonist
inanimate	annoyed	antagonistic
reanimate	annual	antecedent
animus	annually	antechamber
animosity	annuals	antedate
ankle	annuity	antediluvian
annals	perennial	antelope
annalist	semiannual	antenna
annexation	superannuate	antepenult
annihilate	annular	anterior
annihilation	anodyne	anteroom
anniversary	anoint	anthology
anno Domini	anomaly	anthracite
annotate	anomalous	anthrax
annotation	anonymous	anthropoid
announce	anonymity	anthropology
announced	another	antic
announcement	answer	anticipate
announcer	answerable	anticipation
annunciation	answered	anticipatory
annunciator	answers	unanticipated
denounce	unanswerable	anticlimax
pronounce	ant	antidote
unannounced	antagonize	antilogy
annoy	antagonism	antimony

antipathy	apartment	apothegm
antiphonal	compartment	apotheosis
antipodes	department	appanage
antique	apathy	apparatus
antiquarian	apathetic	apparatuses
antiquary	aperture	apparel
antiquated	apex	appeal
antiquity	aphasia	appellant
antisepsis	aphorism	appellate
antiseptic	apiary	appear
antithesis	apocalypse	apparent
antitoxin	apocope	apparition
antler	apocrypha	appearance
antonym	apogee	disappear
anvil	apology	appeasable
anxious	apologetic	unappeasable
anxiety	apologies	append
any	apologist	appendage
anyhow	apologize	appendix
anyone	apoplexy	appendicitis
anything	apostasy	apperceive
anyway	apostolic	apperception
anywhere	apostrophe	appertain
aorta	apostrophize	appurtenance
apart	apothecary	appurtenant

appetite	depreciate	apricot
appetizing	apprehend	apropos
apply	apprehended	apt
appliance	apprehension	aptitude
applicability	apprehensive	aptly
applicable	misapprehension	aqueous
applicant	apprentice	aquarium
application	apprenticeship	aquatic
applied	approach	aqueduct
appoint	approachable	aquiline
appointee	unapproachable	arabesque
appointees	approbation	arable
appointive	appropriate	arbiter
appointment	appropriately	arbitrage
disappoint	appropriateness	arbitrament
reappoint	appropriation	arbitrary
apportion	inappropriate	arbitrate
reapportionment	misappropriate	arbitration
apposite	unappropriated	arbitrator
apposition	approve	arboreal
appraisal	approval	arbutus
appreciate	approved	arcade
appreciable	disapproved	archaic
appreciation	approximate	archangel
appreciative	approximation	archbishop

archduchy	arithmetical	arranges
archeology	arm	derange
archer	armament	disarrange
archery	armature	rearrange
archipelago	armchair	unarranged
architect	armful	arrest
architectural	armistice	arrive
archives	armor	arrival
arctic	armorer	arrived
antarctic	armorial	arrogance
ardor	armory	arrogant
ardent	armpit	arsenal
arduous	disarmed	arsenic
argon	forearmed	arson
Argonaut	unarmed	art
argue	Armenian	artful
argument	arnica	artfulness
argumentation	aroma	artless
argumentative	aromatic	artlessness
arid	arouse	artery
aridity	aroused	arterial
aristocrat	arpeggio	arteriosclerosis
aristocracy	arraignment	arthritis
aristocratic	arrange	artichoke
arithmetic	arrangement	article

articulate	ascetic	aspire
disarticulate	asceticism	aspirant
inarticulate	ascribe	aspirate
artifice	ascribable	aspiration
artificer	ascription	aspirin
artificial	aseptic	assail
artficiality	ashamed	assailable
artillery	ashy	assailant
artisan	Asiatic	unassailable
artist	aside	unassailed
artistic	asinine	assassin
artistry	asininity	assassinate
inartistic	ask	assassination
Aryan	asked	assault
asbestos	unasked	assemble
ascend	askance	assemblage
ascendancy	asleep	assembly
ascendant	asparagus	assert
ascension	aspect	assertion
ascent	asperity	assertive
descend	asperse	assess
ascertain	aspersion	assessable
ascertainable	asphalt	assessed
ascertained	asphyxiate	assesses
ascertainment	asphyxiation	assessment

assessor	dissociate	astronomer
asseverate	assonance	astronomic
assiduous	assort	astute
assiduity	assorted	asylum
assign	assortment	atavism
assignable	assuage	atheism
assignat	assume	atheist
assigned	assumption	athlete
assignee	unassuming	athletic
assignment	assure	athletics
assignor	assurance	athwart
unassigned	assured	Atlantic
assimilate	assures	atmosphere
assimilable	reassure	atmospheric
assimilation	asterisk	atom
assimilative	asthma	atomic
unassimilated	astigmatism	atomize
assist	astonish	atone
assistance	astonished	atoned
assistant	astonishment	atonement
unassisted	astound	unatoned
assize	astrakhan	atrocious
associate	astringent	atrophy
association	astrology	attach
associative	astronomy	attached

attaches	attire	augury
attachment	attired	august
unattached	attitude	augustly
attain	attorney	August
attainable	attract	aureole
attained	attracted	aurora
attainment	attraction	auscultation
unattainable	attractive	auspices
attainder	unattractive	auspicious
attempt	attribute	inauspicious
attempted	auburn	austere
attend	auctioneer	austerity
attendance	audacious	authentic
attendant	audacity	authentically
attended	audible	authenticate
attention	audibility	authenticity
attentive	inaudible	unauthenticated
inattention	audience	author
inattentive	audit	authoritative
unattended	audition	authority
attenuate	auditor	authorization
attenuated	auditorium	authorize
attenuation	auditory	authorship
attest	augment	unauthorized
attestation	augmentative	autobiography

autochthonous	unavailable	avoidable
autocrat	avalanche	avoidance
autocracy	avarice	avoids
autocratic	avaricious	unavoidable
autograph	avenge	avoirdupois
autographed	avenue	avowal
automatic	aver	disavowal
automatism	average	aware
automaton	averse	unaware
automobile	aversion	awful
autonomy	avert	awkward
autopsy	aviation	awning
autosuggestion	aviator	axiom
autumn	avid	axiomatic
autumnal	avidity	axis
auxiliary	avidly	axle
available	avoid	azure

B

babbitt
babble
baccalaureate
bachelor
bacillus
bacilli
back
backbone
backer
background
backhand
backslider
backward
backwardness
backwash
bacterium
bacteria
bacterial
bacteriology
badinage
baffle
bag
bagasse
bagatelle

baggage
bagpipe
bail
bailiff
bailiwick
bailment
balance
unbalanced
balbriggan
balcony
baldachin
baldric
balk
ballast
unballasted
ballet
ballistics
balloon
ballot
balsam
baluster
balustrade
bamboo
banal
banality

banana
bandage
bandaged
bandanna
bandit
bandoleer
bang
banish
banishment
banister
bank
bankrupt
bankruptcy
banquet
banter
baptize
baptism
Baptist
bar
barred
barb
barbed
barbarian
barbaric
barbarism

barbarity	barrier	beatitude
barbarous	barrister	beauty
barbecue	base	beauteous
barber	basal	beauties
barbican	baseboard	beautiful
bargain	basement	beautify
bargained	bases	beaver
barge	basic	because, cause
baritone	basis	bed
barley	debase	bedchamber
barnacle	bashful	bedridden
barograph	bashfulness	bedroom
barometer	basilica	bedspread
barometric	basilisk	bee
baron	bassoon	befall
baroness	baton	befell
baronet	battalion	befit
baronial	battery	before
barrack	battle	beforehand
barrage	bayonet	befriend
barratry	bayou	beg
barrel	beacon	beggar
barren	beagle	begonia
barrenness	beatify	beguile
barricade	beatification	behalf

behave	belligerent	bereave
behaved	bellows	berth
behavior	belong	beseech
misbehave	belove	beside
behead	below	besiege
beheld	belt	bespeak
behest	bench	best
behind	beneath	bestial
behindhand	benediction	bestiality
behold	benefit	bestow
behoove	benefaction	bestowal
beige	benefactor	betray
belfry	beneficence	betrayal
belie	beneficent	betrayed
belief	beneficial	betroth
believable	beneficiary	betrothal
believes	benevolence	better
disbelieve	benevolent	bettered
unbelievable	malevolent	betterment
belittle	benign	between
bell	benignancy	bevel
bellicose	benignant	beveled
bellicosity	benzene	beverage
belligerence	bequeath	bewail
belligerency	bequest	beware

bewilder	binary	blacken
bewilderment	binnacle	blackened
bewitch	binocular	blackmail
beyond	biography	blackness
biannual	biology	blame
bibliography	biplane	blamed
bicameral	birth	blameless
biceps	birthday	blameworthy
bicuspid	birthmark	blandish
bicycle	rebirth	blandishment
bid	bisect	blanket
bidden	bishop	blaspheme
biennial	archbishop	blazon
bigamy	bishopric	blemish
bigot	bismuth	unblemished
bigotry	bison	blight
bijou	bite	blighted
bilingual	bit	blinder
bilious	bitten	blinker
bill, built	bitter	bliss
billboard	bitterest	blissful
billhead	bitumen	blissfully
billiards	black	blissfulness
billow	blackberry	blister
bimetallism	blackboard	blistered

blithesome	boast	bonus
blizzard	boastful	book
block	bodice	bookkeeper
blockade	bodkin	bookkeeping
blockhouse	body	booklet
blood	bodies	bookshelf
bloodless	bodily	boomerang
bloodshot	bodyguard	boracic
bloody	disembodied	border
blouse	embody	bordered
bludgeon	bog	borderless
bluff	bogus	borough
blunder	boiler	borrow
blundered	bold	bosom
blunderer	bolder	botany
blunt	boldest	botanic
blur	bolster	botanical
blush	bolt	botanist
unblushing	bolted	both
bluster	bombardment	bother
boa	bombastic	bothered
boar	bond	bothersome
board	bondage	bottle
boarded	bonded	bottled
boarder	bonnet	bottom

bough	braggart	brigand
boulevard	brandish	brigantine
bounce	brave	bright
bounced	bravery	brighten
bound	bravest	brighter
boundary	brazen	brightly
bounden	brazier	brightness
boundless	breadth	brilliant
unbounded	break	brilliance
bounty	breakable	brilliancy
bounteous	breakage	brilliantine
bounties	unbreakable	bristle
bountiful	unbroken	brocade
bouquet	breast	brochure
bovine	breath	brokerage
bower	brevet	bronchitis
bowlder	breviary	brother
bowsprit	brew	brother-in-law
box	bribery	brotherly
boxed	bride	brougham
boxer	bridal	brown
boxes	brief	brownish
boycott	abbreviate	brunt
bracelet	brevity	brush
brackish	brigade	brute

brutality	bulletin	burlesque
brutalization	bullion	burly
brutalize	bullock	burn
brutally	bulrush	burned
brutish	bulwark	burner
bubble	bunch	burnt
buccaneer	bundle	burnish
bucket	bungalow	burrow
buckle	bungle	bursar
buckler	bunion	burst
buckram	bunker	bury
bucolic	buoy	burial
budget	buoyancy	bush
buffalo	buoyant	business
buffet	burden	businesslike
bugle	burdened	bust
build	burdensome	bustle
builded	bureau	bustled
builder	bureaucracy	busy
built	bureaucrat	busied
bulb	bureaucratic	busily
bulge	burgess	but
bulk	burglar	butcher
bulky	burglarious	butler
bullet	burlap	butt

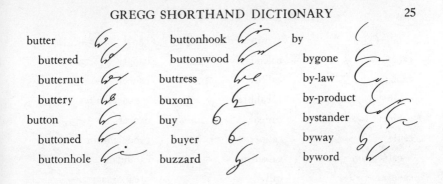

butter	buttonhook	by
buttered	buttonwood	bygone
butternut	buttress	by-law
buttery	buxom	by-product
button	buy	bystander
buttoned	buyer	byway
buttonhole	buzzard	byword

C

cabal	miscalculate	canal
cabbage	calendar	canary
cabin	caliber	cancel
cabinet	calibrate	cancellation
cable	calico	cancer
cablegram	caliper	candelabrum
cadaver	calisthenics	candidate
cadence	call	candidacy
cadenza	recall	candidature
cadet	calliope	candle
caduceus	callous	candor
cafeteria	callosity	candid
caisson	calm	candy
cajole	calmed	candied
calamity	calmly	canine
calamitous	calmness	canister
calcium	calorie	canker
calcimine	calumny	canned
calcine	calumniate	cannery
calculate	calumnious	cannibal
calculable	cambric	cannon
calculation	camel	cannonade
calculator	campaign	cannoneer
incalculable	camphor	canny
	Canadian	canoe

canopy	recapitulate	carburetor
cantaloupe	caprice	carcass
canteen	capricious	carcinoma
canter	capsize	cardboard
cantilever	capstan	cardiac
canton	capsule	cardinal
canvas	captain	care
caoutchouc	caption	careful
capable	captious	careless
capability	capture	carelessness
capacious	captivate	cares
capacitate	captivity	careworn
capacity	captor	career
incapable	carat	caress
incapacitate	caravan	caribou
incapacity	carbide	caricature
capillary	carbine	carmine
capillarity	carbolic	carnal
capital	carbon	carnage
capitalism	bicarbonate	carnival
capitalist	carbohydrate	carnivorous
capitalization	carbonic	incarnate
capitalize	carbonization	incarnation
capitally	carbonize	carol
capitulate	carborundum	carom

carouse		castigate		cathedral	
carp		castigated		catholic	
carpenter		castigation		catholicism	
carpet		casual		catholicity	
carriage		casually		non-catholic	
carrion		casualty		caucus	
carrot		casuist		cauliflower	
carry		cataclysm		cause, because	
carrier		catafalque		causal	
carries		catalepsy		causation	
cartage		catalogue		causative	
cartilage		catalysis		causes	
carton		catamount		caustic	
cartoon		catapult		cauterize	
cartouche		cataract		cauterization	
cartridge		catarrh		caution	
carve		catarrhal		cautionary	
caryatid		catastrophe		cautioned	
cascade		catastrophic		cautious	
cash		catechism		precaution	
cashable		catechize		cavalry	
cashed		category		cavalcade	
cashier		categorical		cavalier	
casino		catenary		cavern	
casserole		caterpillar		caviar	

cavil	celerity	center
cavity	accelerate	centigrade
cease	deceleration	centipede
ceased	celery	central
ceaseless	celestial	centralization
ceases	cellar	centralize
cessation	cello	decentralize
incessant	cellular	centrifugal
unceasing	celluloid	centripetal
cedar	cement	century
cede	cemetery	ceramic
accede	cenotaph	cerebellum
ceded	censer	cerebral
exceed	censor	cerement
intercede	censorious	ceremony
precede	censorship	ceremonial
proceed	uncensored	ceremonious
recede	censure	unceremonious
secede	censurable	certain
succeed	censured	ascertained
cedilla	censures	certainly
celebrate	census	certainty
celebrant	centenary	uncertain
celebration	centenarian	certify
celebrity	centennial	certificate

certification	chandelier	discharge
certiorari	change	chariot
certitude	changeable	charioteer
cessation	changeless	charity
incessant	exchange	charitable
cession	interchangeable	uncharitable
chagrin	unchanged	charlatan
chair	channel	charter
armchair	chant	chartered
chairman	chaos	chassis
chalcedony	chaotic	chasten
chalk	chapel	chastise
challenge	chaperon	chattel
challenger	chaplain	chauffeur
unchallenged	chapter	cheap
chamber	character	cheapen
chamberlain	characteristic	cheapened
chameleon	characterization	cheaper
chamois	characterize	cheapest
champagne	characterizes	cheapness
champion	charcoal	check
championship	charge	cheer
chancel	chargeable	cheered
chancellor	charged	cheerful
chancery	charger	cheerfulness

cheerless	chintz	Christendom
cheery	chipmunk	Christian
chemical	chisel	Christianity
chemist	chiseled	Christmas
chemistry	chivalry	chromatic
cherish	chivalric	achromatic
cherry	chivalrous	panchromatic
cherub	chlorine	chromium
chest	bichloride	chromate
chestnut	chlorate	chromic
chevron	chloride	chronic
chicken	chlorinate	chronicle
chide	chloroform	chronicler
chieftain	chocolate	chronograph
chiffon	choice	chronology
child	choices	chronometer
childhood	choir	chrysanthemum
childish	cholera	chunk
childlike	choose	church
children	chose	churl
grandchild	chosen	churn
chimera	chord	cicatrix
chimeric	chorus	cigar
chimerical	Christ	cigarette
chimney	christen	cincture

cinder	circumspection	uncivilized
incinerate	circumstance	claim
cinematograph	circumstances	acclaim
cinnamon	circumstantial	claimant
cinquefoil	circumstantially	claimed
cipher	circumvent	counterclaim
circle	circus	disclaim
circled	cistern	reclaim
circlet	citadel	unclaimed
encircle	cite	clairvoyance
circuit	citation	clamor
circuitous	incite	clamorous
circular	recite	clandestine
circularization	citizen	clangor
circularize	citizenry	clarify
circulate	citizens	clarification
circulated	citizenship	clarinet
circulation	citric	clarion
circulatory	citron	classic
circumference	civic	classical
circumflex	civil	classicist
circumlocution	civilian	classify
circumnavigate	civility	classification
circumscribe	civilization	unclassified
circumspect	civilize	clavicle

clavier		clerk		closure	
clean		clerical		cloud	
cleaned		clever		cloudless	
cleaner		cleverer		clouds	
cleanest		cleverest		cloudy	
cleanliness		client		unclouded	
cleanness		clientage		clover	
unclean		clientele		clown	
clear		climactic		club	
clearage		climate		clumsy	
clearance		acclimate		clumsier	
cleared		climatic		clumsiest	
clearer		climax		clumsily	
clearest		anticlimax		clumsiness	
clearly		clinic		cluster	
clearness		clinical		clutch	
clears		clinician		clutter	
cleave		clockwise		coach	
cleavage		cloister		coadjutor	
cleaver		close		coagulate	
clement		closed		coal	
clemency		closer		coalesce	
inclement		closest		coalescence	
clergy		disclose		coalescent	
clergyman		closet		coalition	

coarse		coefficient		cohesive	
coarsen		coerce		incoherent	
coarseness		coercion		cohort	
coarser		coercive		coiffure	
coarsest		coeval		coinage	
coast		coexecutor		coincide	
coastal		coffee		coincidence	
coastwise		coffer		coincident	
co-author		coffin		coincidental	
cobalt		cog		colander	
cobble		cogent		coliseum	
cobweb		cogency		collaborate	
cocaine		cogitate		collaboration	
cochineal		cogitation		collaborator	
cockade		cogitative		collapse	
cocktail		cognac		collapsible	
cocoa		cognate		collar	
coconut		cognizant		collate	
cocoon		cognizance		collation	
codefendant		cognomen		collateral	
codfish		cohere		colleague	
codicil		coherence		collect	
codify		coherent		collectible	
codification		coherer		collection	
coeducation		cohesion		collective	

collectorship	colossus	comic
uncollectible	colporteur	comical
college	column	comity
collegiate	columnar	comma
collide	coma	command
collision	comatose	commandant
collodion	combat	commandeer
colloid	combatant	commander
colloquy	combative	commandment
colloquial	non-combatant	commemorate
colloquialism	combine	commemoration
collusion	combination	commemorative
cologne	combined	commence
colonel	combines	commenced
colonnade	combustion	commencement
colony	combustibility	commend
colonial	come	commendable
colonist	comedy	commendation
colonization	comedian	commendatory
colonize	comet	commended
colophon	comfort	commensurate
color	comfortable	commensurable
colorless	comforter	comment
discolor	discomfort	commentary
colossal	uncomfortable	commentator

commented	communion	incomparable
commerce	communism	compartment
commercial	community	apartment
commercialism	communicate	department
commercialization	communicable	compass
commercialize	communicant	compassion
commiserate	communication	compassionate
commiseration	communicative	compatibility
commission	excommunicate	compatible
commissioned	uncommunicative	incompatible
commissioner	commute	compatriot
commissioners	commutation	compel
commit	commuter	compelled
commitment	compact	compulsion
committee	compactness	compulsory
commodious	companion	compendium
commodity	companionable	compendious
commodore	companionship	compensate
common	company	compensation
commoner	accompany	compensatory
commonly	compare	compete
commonwealth	comparable	competed
commotion	comparative	competes
commune	compared	competition
communal	comparison	competitive

competitor	complication	comprehensive
competent	complicity	incomprehensible
competence	accomplice	compress
competently	compliment	compressible
incompetent	complimentary	compression
compile	uncomplimentary	compressor
compilation	complin	comprise
compiled	comply	comprised
complacent	compliance	compromise
complacence	compliant	compromised
complacency	component	comptroller
complain	comport	compulsion
complainant	compose	compulsory
complaint	composedly	compunction
complaisant	composer	compute
complement	composes	computation
complete	composite	computes
completion	composition	comrade
incomplete	compositor	comradeship
uncompleted	composure	concatenate
complex	compound	concatenation
complexity	comprehend	concave
complexion	comprehended	concavity
complicate	comprehensible	conceal
complicated	comprehension	concealed

concealment	conciliatory	condemnatory
concede	irreconcilable	condemned
conceded	reconcile	condense
concession	reconciliation	condensation
conceit	concise	condensed
conceited	conciseness	condenser
conceive	conclave	condenses
conceivable	conclude	condescend
concentrate	conclusion	condescended
concentrated	conclusive	condescension
concentration	inconclusive	condign
concentric	concoct	condiment
concept	concocted	condition
conception	concoction	conditional
concern	concomitant	conditionally
concerned	concord	recondition
unconcerned	concordance	unconditional
concert	discord	condolence
concerted	concourse	condone
disconcerted	concrete	condonation
preconcerted	concur	conduce
concession	concurrence	conducive
conch	concurrent	conduct
conciliate	condemn	conducted
conciliation	condemnation	conductivity

conductor	confidentially	confounded
misconduct	confidently	confront
conduit	confine	confronted
cone	confined	confuse
conic	confinement	confused
conical	unconfined	confuses
confection	confirm	confusion
confectioner	affirm	confute
confectionery	confirmation	confutation
confederate	confirmed	congeal
confederacy	unconfirmed	congealed
confederation	confiscate	congenial
confer	confiscated	congeniality
conferee	confiscation	uncongeniality
conference	confiscatory	congest
conferred	conflagration	congested
confess	conflict	congestion
confession	confliction	congests
confessional	confluence	conglomerate
confessor	conform	conglomeration
confide	conformable	congratulate
confidant	conformation	congratulated
confidence	conformed	congratulation
confident	conformity	congratulatory
confidential	confound	congregate

congregated

congregation

congregational

gregarious

segregate

congress

congressional

congruous

incongruous

conjecture

conjectural

conjugal

conjugate

conjugated

conjugation

conjunction

conjuncture

conjure

conjured

conjurer

conjures

connect

connected

connection

connective

disconnected

unconnected

connivance

connoisseur

connotation

conquer

conqueror

unconquerable

unconquered

conquest

conquests

consanguinity

conscience

conscientious

conscious

consciousness

unconscious

conscript

conscription

consecrate

consecrated

consecration

unconsecrated

consecutive

consensus

consent

consented

consequence

consequent

consequential

inconsequential

conserve

conservation

conservatism

conservative

conservatory

conserved

consider

considerable

considerate

consideration

considers

inconsiderate

unconsidered

consign

consigned

consignee

consignment

consignor

consist

consistence	constant	consult
consistency	constancy	consultant
consistent	constellation	consultation
consists	consternation	consults
inconsistent	constitute	consume
console	constituency	consumed
consolation	constituent	consumer
consoles	constitution	consummate
disconsolate	constitutional	consummation
inconsolable	constitutionality	consumption
consolidate	constitutionally	consumptive
consolidated	unconstitutional	contact
consolidation	constrain	contagion
consonant	constraint	contagious
consonance	unconstrained	contain
consort	constrict	contained
consorted	constrictor	container
conspicuous	construct	contaminate
conspicuously	constructed	contamination
inconspicuous	constructive	uncontaminated
conspire	misconstruction	contemplate
conspiracy	construe	contemplated
conspirator	construed	contemplation
constable	consul	contemplative
constabulary	consulate	contemporaneous

contemporary

contempt

contemptible

contemptuous

contend

contended

contention

content

contented

contentment

discontented

contest

contestant

contestation

contested

contests

incontestable

context

contiguous

contiguity

continent

continental

contingent

contingency

continue

continual

continually

continuance

continuation

continued

continuity

continuous

discontinue

contort

contorted

contortion

contour

contraband

contract

contracted

contraction

contractor

contradict

contradiction

contradictory

uncontradicted

contradistinction

contraption

contrary

contrariness

contrast

contrasted

contravene

contravention

contribute

contribution

contributor

contributory

contrite

contrition

contrived

contrivance

control

controlled

controller

uncontrollable

controvert

controversial

controversy

incontroverted

incontrovertible

contumacy

contumacious

contumely

contused

contusion	converses	convulsive
conundrum	convert	cookery
convalescence	conversion	cooperate
convalescent	converted	cooperation
convection	convertible	cooperative
convene	convex	coordinate
convention	convexity	coordination
reconvene	convey	copartnership
convenience	conveyance	copious
conveniences	conveyed	copper
convenient	conveyer	copy
inconvenienced	convict	copyist
inconvenient	conviction	copyright
convent	convince	cordage
conventual	convinced	cordial
convention	convivial	cordiality
conventional	conviviality	corduroy
unconventional	convoke	cork
converge	convocation	corn
convergent	convoked	cornstarch
converse	convolution	corner
conversant	convoy	cornet
conversation	convoyed	cornice
conversational	convulse	corona
conversed	convulsion	coroner

coronet	correspond	cosmetic
coronation	correspondence	cosmic
corporal	correspondent	cosmopolitan
corporate	corresponds	cost
corporately	corridor	costliness
corporation	corroborate	costly
incorporate	corroboration	costume
corporeal	corroborative	costumed
corps	uncorroborated	costumer
corpse	corrode	cosy
corpulence	corrosion	cosily
corpuscle	corrosive	cosiness
correct	corrugate	cotemporaneous
corrected	corrugation	contemporaneous
correction	corrupt	coterie
corrective	corruption	cottage
correctly	corruptly	cotton
correctness	incorruptible	couch
corrector	corset	cougar
incorrect	cortex	could
uncorrected	corundum	council
correlate	carborundum	councilor
correlated	coruscate	count
correlation	coruscation	counted
correlative	coryza	countess

countless	courageous	recover
uncounted	discourage	uncover
countenance	encouragement	covert
discountenance	courier	covetous
counter	course	coward
counteract	concourse	cowardice
counterbalance	courser	cowboy
counterclaim	courses	cowl
counterfeit	discourse	coxswain
counterfeited	discursive	cracker
counterirritant	recourse	cranberry
countermand	court	cranium
countermanded	courted	cranial
countermine	courthouse	craziness
countermined	courtliness	create
counterpart	court-martial	created
counterpoint	courtyard	creation
country	courteous	creative
countryside	courtesy	creator
county	cousin	creature
coupé	covenant	recreation
couple	cover	credence
coupled	coverlet	credential
coupon	discover	credible
courage	discovery	credibility

credulity	cripple	coronet
credulous	crisis	crowned
incredible	crises	crucial
incredulity	criterion	crucible
incredulous	criteria	crucifix
credit	critic	crucifixion
creditable	criticism	crucify
creditor	criticize	crude
credits	criticizes	crudely
discreditable	critics	crudity
cremate	crochet	cruel
cremation	crocodile	cruelly
crematory	crocus	cruelty
creole	crop	cruise
creosote	croquet	cruised
crescendo	crosier	cruiser
crescent	cross	cruises
crestfallen	crossed	crumb
cretonne	crosses	crumble
crevice	crossroad	crumple
crew	crouch	crusade
cribbage	crowd	crusader
criminal	crowded	crutch
crimson	crowds	crux
crinoline	crown	crypt

cryptic	cultivated	curb
cryptogram	cultivates	curd
crystal	cultivation	cure
crystalline	cultivator	curable
crystallization	uncultivated	curative
crystallize	culture	cures
cube	cultural	incurable
cubed	cultured	curfew
cubic	uncultured	curious
cubical	culvert	curiosity
cuckoo	cumbrous	curiously
cucumber	cumbersome	curl
cudgel	encumber	curly
cuisine	encumbrance	currant
culinary	unencumbered	currency
culminate	cumulative	current
culminated	accumulate	curriculum
culmination	cuneiform	curricula
culpable	cunning	curse
culpability	cupboard	cursive
culprit	cupful	cursory
exculpate	cupidity	curtail
inculpate	cupola	curtain
cult	curate	curve
cultivate	curator	curvature

curved	customs	cylindrical
cushion	cutaneous	cymbal
cushioned	cuticle	cynic
cuspidor	subcutaneous	cynically
custard	cutlery	cynicism
custody	cutlet	cynosure
custodian	cycle	cyst
custom	cyclone	cystoid
accustomed	cyclopedia	czar
customary	cyclopedic	czarina
customer	encyclopedia	czarism
customhouse	cylinder	Czech

D

dachshund	dangerous	daylight
daffodil	dangers	days
daguerreotype	endangered	daytime
dainty	dare	dazzle
daintier	dared	dazzled
daintiest	dares	dead
daintily	dark	deaden
dalliance	darken	deadened
damage	darkness	deadeye
damaged	data	deadfall
indemnify	datum	deadliness
undamaged	date	deaf
damask	dated	deafened
damp	undated	deafness
dampen	dative	deal
dampener	daughter	dealer
damper	daughter-in-law	deals
dampness	granddaughter	dealt
dance	daunt	dear
danced	dauntless	dearer
dancer	undaunted	dearest
dandelion	davenport	dearly
dandy	davit	dears
danger	day	deary
	daydream	endeared

dearth	decanter	decisiveness
death	decapitate	indecision
deathbed	decapitation	undecided
deathless	decathlon	decimal
deathlike	decease	decimate
deathly	deceased	decipher
debacle	decedent	decipherable
debate	deceit	undecipherable
debatable	deceitful	declaim
debated	deceive	declamation
debater	deceiver	declamatory
debenture	deceives	declare
debilitate	deception	declarable
debilitated	deceptive	declaration
debilitation	decent	declarative
debility	decency	declaratory
debonair	decently	decline
debt	indecency	declension
debit	indecent	declined
debtor	decide	declivity
indebtedness	decidedly	incline
début	decides	recline
decade	decision	decoction
decadence	decisive	decompose
decalcomania	decisively	decomposed

decomposition	deed	defendant
decorate	deeded	defended
decoration	misdeed	defender
decorative	deep	defense
decorator	deepen	defenseless
decorum	deepness	defensible
decorous	depth	defensive
decoy	deer	defer
decoyed	deface	deference
decrease	efface	deferential
decreased	defalcate	deficiency
decree	defalcation	deficient
decrepit	defalcator	deficit
decrepitude	defame	defile
dedicate	defamation	define
dedication	defamatory	definable
dedicator	default	definite
dedicatory	defaulted	definiteness
deduce	defaulter	definition
deduces	defeat	definitive
deducible	defeated	indefinable
deduct	defect	indefinitely
deductible	defection	deflate
deduction	defective	deflation
deductively	defend	deform

deformed	deity	delineation
deformity	deject	delineator
defraud	dejectedly	delinquent
defrauded	dejection	delinquency
defray	delay	delirium
defrayal	delectable	delirious
deft	delectation	deliver
defunct	delegate	deliverable
defy	delegation	deliverance
defiance	delete	deliverer
defiant	deletion	delivery
defied	deleterious	undeliverable
degenerate	deliberate	delude
degeneracy	deliberately	deluded
degeneration	deliberation	delusion
degrade	deliberative	delusive
degradation	delicate	deluge
degraded	delicacy	demagogue
degree	delicatessen	demand
dehydrate	indelicate	demarcation
deify	delicious	demeanor
deification	delight	demented
deifies	delighted	dementia
deism	delightful	demerit
deist	delineate	demise

demobilize	denizen	compartment
demobilization	denominate	department
demobilized	denominated	departmental
democrat	denomination	departure
democracy	denominator	depend
democratic	denote	dependable
democratically	denounce	depended
demolish	denouncement	dependence
demolition	denouncer	dependent
demon	denunciation	independence
demonetize	denunciatory	independent
demonetization	dense	depict
demonstrate	density	depicted
demonstrable	dental	deplete
demonstrative	dentist	depleted
demonstrator	dentistry	depletion
demoralize	deny	deplore
demoralization	denial	deplorability
demoralized	denied	deplorable
dcmur	denier	deponent
demurrer	denies	depopulate
demurrage	undeniable	deport
demure	deodorize	deportation
denature	depart	deported
denim	apartment	deportment

depose	depute	descriptive
deposes	deputation	desecrate
deposit	deputize	desecration
depositary	deputy	desert
deposition	derange	deserted
depositor	derangement	deserter
depository	derelict	desertion
depot	dereliction	deserve
deprave	deride	deservedly
depravation	derision	undeserved
depravity	derisive	desiccate
deprecate	derive	desiccation
deprecation	derivation	desiccator
deprecatory	derivative	design
depreciate	derogation	designate
depreciation	derogative	designation
depredation	derogatory	designed
depress	derrick	designer
depressant	descend	desire
depression	ascend	desirable
depressive	descendant	desires
deprive	descent	desirous
deprivation	describe	undesirable
privation	describable	desist
depth	description	desisted

desists	destroy	determine
desolate	destroyed	determination
desolately	destroyer	determinedly
desolation	destruction	indeterminate
despair	destructive	predetermined
despaired	desuetude	undetermined
desperate	desultory	detest
desperately	desultorily	detestable
desperation	detach	detestation
despise	detached	dethrone
despicable	detachment	dethroned
despite	detail	detonate
despond	detailed	detonation
despondency	detain	detour
despondent	detained	detract
despot	detention	detraction
despotic	detect	detractor
despotism	detected	detriment
dessert	detective	detrimental
destine	detector	devastate
destination	deter	devastation
destined	deterrent	develop
destiny	deteriorate	developer
destitute	deteriorated	development
destitution	deterioration	undeveloped

deviate	diagnostic	dictograph
deviated	diagnostician	dictum
deviation	diagonal	dicta
devious	diagonally	dictums
device	diagram	didactic
devised	diagrammatic	diet
devil	dialect	dietary
devoid	dialectics	dietetics
devolve	dialogue	differ
devote	diameter	difference
devotee	diametric	different
devotion	diametrically	differential
devotional	diamond	differentially
devout	diapason	differentiate
dexterous	diaphanous	differentiation
ambidextrous	diaphragm	differently
dexterity	diatribe	indifferent
diabetes	dictaphone	difficult
diabetic	dictate	difficulties
diabolical	dictation	difficulty
diacritical	dictator	diffident
diadem	dictatorial	diffidence
diaeresis	dictatorially	diffraction
diagnose	diction	diffuse
diagnosis	dictionary	diffuses

diffusible	dilemma	dingy
diffusion	diligent	dinosaur
digest	diligence	dint
digestible	dilute	diocese
digestion	diluted	diphtheria
digestive	dilution	diphtheritic
indigestion	undiluted	diphthong
undigested	dim	diphthongal
digit	dimly	diploma
digital	dimmed	diplomat
digitalis	dimmer	diplomacy
dignify	dimness	diplomatic
dignitary	undimmed	diplomatist
dignity	dimension	dipsomania
indignity	dimensional	dipsomaniac
undignified	diminish	dire
digress	diminuendo	direful
digression	diminution	dircly
digressive	diminutive	direct
dike	undiminished	direction
dilapidate	dimity	directness
dilapidation	dimple	director
dilate	dine	directorate
dilation	dined	directory
dilatory	dinner	indirect

undirected	disastrous	discolor
dirigible	disavow	discoloration
disable	disavowal	discomfiture
disability	disband	discomfort
disabuse	disbelieve	discompose
disadvantage	disbeliever	discomposes
disadvantageous	disbursement	discomposure
disaffected	discard	disconcert
disaffection	discarded	disconcertedly
disagree	discern	discontent
disagreeable	discernible	discontented
disagreed	discernment	discontinue
disagreement	discharge	discontinuance
disallow	discharged	discontinued
disappear	disciple	discord
disappearance	disciplinary	concord
disappoint	discipline	discordant
disappointment	disclaim	discount
disapprobation	disclaimed	discountenance
disapprove	disclaimer	discourage
disapproval	disclose	discouraged
disarm	disclosed	discouragement
disarrange	discloses	encourage
disarticulate	disclosure	discourse
disaster	undisclosed	discursive

discourteous	disentangle	disinherit
discover	disfavor	disintegrate
discoverer	disfeature	disinterested
discovery	disfigure	disjoin
discreditable	disfranchise	disjunction
discreet	disgrace	disjunctive
discretion	disgraceful	dislike
indiscreet	disguise	dislocate
discrepancy	undisguised	dislodge
discriminate	disgust	disloyal
discriminated	dishabille	dismal
discrimination	dishearten	dismantle
discriminatory	dishevel	dismay
indiscriminate	dishonor	undismayed
discuss	dishonest	dismember
discussion	dishonestly	dismiss
disdain	dishonesty	dismissal
disdained	dishonorable	dismissed
disdainful	disillusion	dismount
diseased	disincline	disobey
disembark	disinclination	disobedience
disembarcation	disinclined	disobedient
disenchant	disinfect	disobeyed
disengage	disinfectant	disoblige
disengagement	disingenuous	disorderly

disorganize

disparage

disparagement

disparate

disparity

dispassionate

dispatch

dispatched

dispatcher

dispel

dispelled

dispense

dispensable

dispensary

dispensation

dispensed

disperse

dispersal

dispersion

displacement

disport

dispose

disposal

disposes

disposition

dispossess

disproportion

disproportionate

disprove

disproof

dispute

disputation

disputatious

disputes

undisputed

disqualify

disqualification

disquisition

disregard

disrepute

disreputable

disrespect

disrupt

disruption

dissatisfy

dissatisfaction

dissect

dissection

dissemble

disseminate

dissemination

dissent

dissension

dissented

dissenter

dissertation

dissidence

dissimilar

dissimilarity

dissimulate

dissipate

dissociate

dissolute

dissoluble

dissolution

indissoluble

dissonant

dissonance

dissuade

dissuasion

persuade

suasion

distant

distance

distaste

distasteful	distributive	diversification
distend	distributor	diversify
distensible	redistribute	diversion
distension	undistributed	diversity
distill	district	divert
distillate	redistricted	divest
distillation	distrust	divide
distillery	distrusted	divided
distinct	distrustful	dividend
distinction	disturb	divider
distinctive	disturbance	divisible
distinguish	disturbed	division
distinguishable	disturber	divisor
indistinct	undisturbed	indivisible
indistinguishable	disuse	undivided
distort	ditto	divine
distorted	diurnal	divination
distortion	divagate	divined
distract	divagation	divinity
distrain	divan	divorce
distraught	diverge	divorcée
distress	divergence	divulge
distressed	divergent	dizzy
distribute	divers	dizzily
distribution	diverse	dizziness

docile	dominant	dower
docility	domination	dowager
docket	domineer	down
dockyard	dominion	downcast
doctor	predominate	downfall
doctorate	domino	downright
doctrine	donate	downward
doctrinaire	donated	doxology
doctrinal	donation	dozen
document	donor	draft
documentary	donkey	dragon
doge	door	dragoon
dogma	doorway	drainage
dogmatic	dooryard	drama
dogmatize	dormant	dramatic
doldrums	dormer	dramatist
dollar	dormitory	dramatization
domain	dormouse	dramatize
domestic	double	drapery
domesticate	doubt	drastic
domesticated	doubted	draw
domesticity	doubtful	drawback
domicile	doubtless	drawbridge
dominate	doubts	drawee
dominance	undoubted	drawer

drawn	drunken	duplicator
dread	drunkenness	duplicity
dreaded	dry	durable
dreadful	drier	durability
dreadnaught	driest	during
dream	dryly	duration
dreamed	dryness	dust
dreamer	dry-shod	duty
dreamily	dual	duteous
drift	dubiety	dutiable
driveway	dubious	duties
dromedary	indubitable	dutiful
droop	duchess	undutiful
drop	ductile	dwarf
drought	ductility	dwell
drown	duel	dwelt
drowned	duly	dwindle
drudge	unduly	dwindled
drudgery	dumb	dynamic
drug	dump	dynamite
druggist	dungeon	dynamo
drum	duplex	dynasty
drunk	duplicate	dyspepsia
drunkard	duplication	dyspeptic

E

each	easier	eclipsed
eager	easiest	economy
eagerly	easily	economic
eagerness	easiness	economical
ear	uneasiness	economist
eardrum	uneasy	economize
earmark	east	ecstasy
earldom	eastern	ecstatic
early	easterner	eczema
earlier	eastward	edible
earliest	eat	edibility
earnest	eatable	inedible
earnestly	eaten	edifice
earnestness	eater	edification
earth	uneaten	edify
earthen	ebony	edit
earthenware	ebullient	edition
earthliness	ebullience	editor
earthquake	ebullition	editorial
earthward	eccentric	editorially
earthwork	eccentricity	unedited
earthworm	ecclesiastic	educate
unearth	éclat	education
ease	eclectic	educational
	eclipse	educator

uneducated	effort	elaboration
efface	effortless	elastic
deface	effrontery	elasticity
effacement	effulgent	elect
effect	effusion	election
effective	effusive	electioneer
effectual	ego	elective
effectually	egoism	elector
effectuate	egoist	electoral
effectuation	egotism	electorate
ineffectual	egotist	reelect
effeminate	egotistic	electric
effeminacy	egregious	electrical
effervesce	egress	electrician
effervescence	congress	electricity
effervescent	ingress	electrification
efficacious	progress	electrify
efficacy	transgress	electrocute
efficient	either	electrode
efficiency	ejaculate	electrolier
inefficiency	eject	electrolysis
inefficient	ejection	electrolyte
efflorescent	inject	electromagnet
efflux	reject	electron
influx	elaborate	electroplate

electrotype	eliminated	emaciate
eleemosynary	elimination	emaciated
elegant	eliminative	emaciation
elegance	elite	emanate
elegantly	elixir	emanated
inelegant	ellipse	emanation
element	ellipsis	emancipate
elemental	ellipsoid	emancipation
elementally	elliptic	emancipator
elementary	elliptical	embankment
elephant	elocution	embargo
elephantine	elocutionist	embarkation
elevate	elongate	embarrass
elevated	elongation	embarrassed
elevation	eloquent	embarrasses
elevator	eloquence	embarrassment
elicit	grandiloquent	embassy
elicitation	else	ambassador
elicited	elsewhere	embezzle
elide	elucidate	embezzled
elision	elucidation	embezzlement
eligible	elude	embezzler
eligibility	elusion	emblem
ineligible	elusive	emblematic
eliminate	elusory	embody

embodies

embodiment

embolden

emboldened

embrace

embroider

embroideries

embroidery

embryonic

emendation

emerald

emerge

emerged

emergence

emergency

emergent

emeritus

emigrate

emigrant

emigration

immigrate

eminent

eminence

eminently

imminent

emissary

emit

emission

emollient

emolument

emotion

emotional

emotionally

unemotional

emperor

empress

emphasis

emphasized

emphasizes

emphatic

empire

empiric

empirical

empiricism

employ

employee

employer

employment

unemployment

emporium

empty

emptied

emptiest

emptiness

emulate

emulous

emulsify

emulsion

enable

inability

unable

enact

enactment

reenact

enamel

enameled

encampment

enchant

enchanted

enchantment

encircle

enclose

enclosure

encomium

encomiastic

encore	unendorsed	engage
encounter	endow	disengage
encountered	endowed	engagement
encounters	endowment	engages
encourage	unendowed	reengage
discourage	endure	engine
encouraged	endurable	engineer
encouragement	endurance	English
encourages	unendurable	engraver
encroachment	enemy	engross
encumbrance	enmity	enhance
encyclical	inimical	enhancement
encyclopedia	energy	unenhanced
encyclopedic	energetic	enigma
end	energize	enigmatic
ended	enfeeble	enjoin
endless	enfold	enjoined
unending	enforce	injunction
endanger	enforceable	enjoy
endangered	enforced	enjoyable
endearment	enforcement	enjoyed
endeavor	enforces	enjoyment
endemic	reenforce	enjoys
endorse	enfranchise	enlarge
endorsement	enfranchisement	enlarged

enlargement	enslave	enthroned
enlighten	ensue	enthusiasm
enlightened	ensued	enthusiast
enlightenment	ensues	enthusiastic
unenlightened	entablature	enthusiastically
enlist	entail	unenthusiastic
enlistment	entailed	entice
enlists	entangle	enticed
reenlists	disentangled	entices
enliven	enter	entire
enmity	entered	entirely
ennoble	enters	entirety
ennoblement	entrance	entitle
ennui	entrant	entity
enormous	entry	entomb
enormity	reenter	entombed
enormously	enterprise	entombment
enough	unenterprising	entomology
enrapture	entertain	entrain
enrich	entertained	entrance
enriched	entertainer	entrap
enrichment	entertainment	entreat
ensconce	enthrall	entrust
ensign	enthralled	entry
ensilage	enthrone	entryway

entwine

entwined

enumerate

enumeration

enumerator

enunciate

enunciation

enunciator

envelope

envelopment

environs

environment

envoy

envy

enviable

envious

unenviable

enzyme

epaulette

ephemeral

ephemerally

epic

epical

epicure

epicurean

epidemic

epidermic

epidermis

epiglottis

epigram

epilepsy

epileptic

epilogue

episcopal

episcopalian

episode

episodic

epistle

epitaph

epithelium

epithet

epitome

epitomize

epoch

epochal

equable

equability

equal

equality

equalization

equalize

equally

unequaled

equanimity

equation

equator

equatorial

equestrian

equiangular

equidistant

equilateral

equilibrium

equilibrist

equine

equinox

equinoctial

equip

equipage

equipment

equity

equitable

inequitable

inequity

equivalent

equivocal

equivocate	erratic	escrow
equivocation	erratum	escutcheon
equivocator	inerrant	especial
eradicate	unerringly	especially
eradicable	errand	espionage
eradication	error	esplanade
ineradicable	erroneous	espouse
erase	erudite	espousal
erasable	erudition	esprit
eraser	erupt	esquire
erasure	eruption	essayist
erect	eruptive	essence
erectile	erysipelas	essential
erectility	escalator	essentially
erection	escapade	quintessence
erectness	escape	establishment
erector	escaped	estate
ergo	escapement	esteem
ermine	inescapable	esteemed
erode	escheat	estimable
erosion	eschew	inestimable
erosive	eschewal	esthetic
err	escort	estimate
aberration	escorted	estimated
errata	unescorted	estimation

estimator	euphemistic	uneventful
estop	euphony	ever
estoppel	evacuate	whatever
estranged	evacuated	whenever
estrangement	evacuation	wherever
estuary	evade	whichever
etch	evaded	every
eternal	evasion	everybody
eternally	evasive	everything
eternity	evaluate	everywhere
ether	evaluated	evict
ethereal	evaluation	eviction
etherealize	evanescent	evident
ethics	evanescence	evidence
ethical	evangelist	evil
unethical	evangelical	evilly
ethnic	evaporate	evince
ethnology	evaporation	evoke
ethyl	evening	evocation
etymology	event	evolve
eucalyptus	eventful	evolution
euchre	eventual	evolutionist
eulogy	eventuality	exacerbation
eulogize	eventually	exact
euphemism	eventuate	exaction

exactitude	excellency	exclude
exactness	excellent	excluded
inexact	excelsior	exclusion
exaggeration	except	exclusive
exalt	exceptionable	include
exaltation	unexceptionable	included
exalted	excerpt	excommunicate
examine	excess	excoriate
examination	excessive	excrescence
example	exchange	excruciate
exemplary	exchangeable	exculpate
exemplification	exchequer	exculpation
exemplify	excise	exculpatory
sample	excision	excursion
unexampled	excite	excuse
exasperate	excitability	excusable
exasperation	excitable	excuses
excavate	excitant	inexcusable
excavation	excitation	execrate
excavator	excitement	execrable
exceed	exciter	execration
exceeded	exclaim	execute
excel	exclaimed	executant
excelled	exclamation	execution
excellence	exclamatory	executioner

executive	exhibition	exorbitant
executor	exhibitor	exordium
executrix	exhilarate	exoteric
exemplify	exhilaration	esoterical
exemplar	exhort	exotic
exemplary	exhortation	expand
exemplification	exhorted	expanse
exempt	exhume	expansible
exemption	exhumation	expansion
exequatur	exhumed	expansive
exercise	inhume	expatiate
exercises	exigent	expatiated
exert	exigency	expatiation
exerted	exiguous	expatriate
exertion	exile	expect
exhale	exiled	expectancy
exhalation	exist	expectant
exhaust	existence	expectation
exhaustible	existent	unexpectedly
exhaustion	exit	expectorate
exhaustive	exodus	expedient
exhaustless	ex officio	expedience
inexhaustible	exonerate	expedite
exhibit	exoneration	expedition
exhibited	exonerative	expeditious

expel	inexplicable	expressible
expelled	explicit	expression
expulsion	explode	expressive
expend	explosion	expressman
expenditure	exploit	unexpressed
expense	exploitation	expropriate
expensive	explore	expropriation
experience	exploration	expulsion
inexperienced	exploratory	expulsive
experiment	exponent	expunge
experimental	exponential	expurgate
experimentation	export	exquisite
experimenter	exportable	extant
expert	exportation	extempore
expiate	exported	extemporaneous
expiation	exporter	extemporary
expiatory	expose	extemporization
expire	exposes	extemporize
expiration	exposition	extend
explain	expositor	extended
explainable	expository	extension
explanation	expostulate	extensive
explanatory	expound	extent
expletive	express	extenuate
explicable	expressage	extenuated

extenuation	extract	extrude
exterior	extractable	exuberant
exterminate	extraction	exuberancy
extermination	extractive	exult
exterminator	extractor	exultant
external	extradite	exultation
externally	extraditible	exulted
extinct	extradition	eye
extinction	extraneous	eyeball
extinguish	extraordinary	eyebar
extinguishable	extraordinarily	eyebrow
extirpate	extravagant	eyeglass
extirpation	extravagance	eyelash
extol	extravaganza	eyelet
extolled	extreme	eyelid
extort	extremist	eyepiece
extorted	extremity	eyes
extortion	extricate	eyesight
extortionate	extrication	eyesore
extra	extrinsic	eyetooth

F

fable	manufacture	infamy
fabulous	Fahrenheit	familiar
fabric	fail	familiarity
fabricate	failed	familiarization
fabrication	failure	familiarize
facade	faith	familiarly
face	faithfulness	unfamiliar
facet	faithless	family
facial	unfaithful	families
facetious	falcon	famine
facile	fall	famish
facilely	fallen	fanatic
facilitate	fallacy	fanaticism
facility	fallacious	fanatics
facsimile	fallible	fancy
fact	infallible	fancier
faction	false	fanciest
factional	falsehood	fanciful
factious	falsification	fantasy
factitious	falsify	fantasia
factor	falsity	fantastic
factory	falter	far
facultative	fame	farsighted
faculty	defame	farther
	famous	farthest

farm	fatherless	feather
farmed	fathom	featherweight
farmers	fatigue	feature
farmhouse	fatuous	disfeature
farmyard	fatuity	febrile
farthing	faucet	federal
fascinate	fault	confederate
fascinated	faultily	federacy
fascination	faultless	federalist
fashion	faulty	federalize
fashionable	favor	federate
old-fashioned	disfavor	federation
unfashionable	favorable	feeble
fast	favorite	enfeeble
fasten	favoritism	feebleness
faster	favors	felicitate
fastest	unfavorable	felicitous
fastidious	fealty	felicity
fatal	fear	feline
fatality	fearful	felon
fatally	fearless	felonious
father	fearsome	felony
fatherhood	feasible	female
father-in-law	feasibility	feminine
fatherland	feast	femininity

femur	festoon	filter
fender	fetish	filtered
ferment	fever	filtration
fermentable	feverish	filth
fermentation	fiasco	final
unfermented	fiat	finalist
ferocious	fiber	finality
ferocity	fibrous	finally
ferric	fickle	finance
ferrous	fiction	financial
ferrule	fictional	financier
fertile	fictitious	find
fertility	fidelity	finder
fertilization	infidel	finds
fertilize	perfidy	finc
fertilizer	fiduciary	fined
fervor	field	fineness
effervesce	fiend	finery
fervency	fiendish	refinery
fervent	figure	finger
fervid	disfigure	fingerling
festal	figurative	finis
festival	figurehead	finish
festive	transfigure	unfinished
festivity	filament	finite

infinite	fit	flannel
infinitesimal	fitful	flash
infinitive	fitly	flashily
infinity	fitness	flashy
fire	fix	flask
fiery	affix	flatiron
firearm	fixation	flatter
firebrand	fixative	flattered
firefly	fixes	flatterer
fireman	fixity	flatters
fire plug	fixture	flattery
fireproof	prefix	flaunt
fireside	suffix	flavor
firm	transfix	flavorous
firmness	flaccid	flaxen
firmament	flagellate	fleet
first	flagrant	flex
fiscal	flagrance	flexibility
fish	flagrancy	flexible
fisherman	flame	flexor
fishery	flamboyant	flexure
fishhook	inflammation	inflexible
fishy	flamingo	flicker
fissure	flange	flight
fist	flank	flighty

flinch	flush	follows
fling	flute	fomentation
flint	flutter	fond
flippant	fluttered	fondest
flirtation	fluttery	fondness
float	fly	fondant
flotation	flight	fondle
flotsam	flyer	fool
flounce	flywheel	foolhardy
flounder	focus	foolish
flour	foci	foolscap
flourish	focuses	foot
flower	fodder	football
florist	foghorn	footboard
fluctuate	foible	footbridge
fluctuated	foil	footgear
fluctuation	foist	foothill
fluent	fold	foothold
fluency	folio	footlights
fluid	foliage	footnote
fluidity	foliation	footpath
fluidrachm	portfolio	footprint
flume	folk	footsore
fluorine	follow	footstep
fluorescent	follower	footstool

for	forefinger	forgetful
forage	foregone	forgettable
forasmuch	foreground	forgot
foray	foreign	unforgettable
forbear	foreigner	forgive
forbearance	foreknowledge	forgave
forbore	foremost	forgivable
forbid	forename	forgiven
forbidden	forenoon	unforgivable
force	foreordain	unforgiven
enforce	forerunner	forgo
forced	forest	fork
forceful	forestry	forlorn
forces	foretell	form
reenforce	foretold	conform
forceps	forethought	deform
forcible	forewoman	formal
forearm	forfeit	formality
forebear	forfeiture	formally
foreboding	forgather	format
forecast	forge	formation
forecaster	forged	formative
forecastle	forger	formerly
foreclose	forgery	informal
foreclosure	forget	uniform

formaldehyde	foul	fraternity
formidable	foulard	fraternal
formula	found	fraternally
formulate	foundation	fraternize
forsake	founded	fraud
forsooth	founder	defrauded
forswear	foundry	fraudulent
forthcoming	fount	free
forthright	fountain	freed
forthwith	foursome	freedom
fortify	fowl	freely
fortification	fox	freeness
fortress	fracas	freight
unfortified	fractional	freighter
fortitude	fracture	frequent
fortnight	fragile	frequency
fortuitous	fragility	frequently
fortune	fragment	fresh
fortunate	fragmentary	freshen
misfortune	frailty	freshly
unfortunate	franchise	freshman
forward	disfranchise	freshness
forwarder	enfranchise	fretwork
fossil	frantic	friable
foster	frenetic	friend

friendless	frosted	fully
friendly	frosty	fulminate
friendship	froth	fulmination
unfriendly	froward	fulsome
frigate	frown	fume
fright	frowned	fumigate
frighten	frugal	fumigation
frightened	fruit	perfume
frightful	fruitful	function
frigid	fruition	functional
frigidity	fruitless	fundamental
frigidly	frustrate	funereal
refrigerator	frustration	fungus
fringe	fuchsia	fungi
frivolity	fudge	funnel
frivolous	fuel	fur
frock	fugitive	furlough
frolic	fugacious	furnace
front	refuge	furnish
frontage	fulcrum	furnisher
frontal	fulfill	furnishings
fronted	fulfillment	furniture
frontier	unfulfilled	unfurnished
frontispiece	full	furor
frost	fullness	further

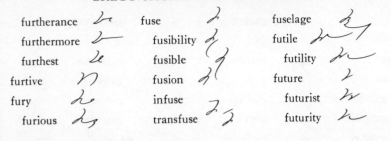

furtherance	fuse	fuselage
furthermore	fusibility	futile
furthest	fusible	futility
furtive	fusion	future
fury	infuse	futurist
furious	transfuse	futurity

G

gable	gangway	gastronomic
gage	gap	gate
gain	garage	gatehouse
gained	garb	gatekeeper
gainful	garbage	gatepost
gainsay	garble	gateway
galaxy	gardener	gather
gall	gargoyle	gathered
gallant	garland	gatherer
gallantry	garlic	gaudy
gallery	garment	gauge
gallon	garner	gauger
gallop	garnet	gauntlet
galvanize	garnish	gauze
galvanism	garnishee	gay
galvanization	garnisher	gayety
gambit	garnishment	gayly
gamble	garniture	gayness
gambled	garrison	gazelle
gambler	garrulous	gazette
gamut	garrulity	gelatin
ganglion	garter	gelatinize
gangrene	gasoline	gelatinoid
gangrenous	gasp	gelatinous
	gastric	gender

genealogy	genteel	gerund
general	gentian	gerundive
generalissimo	Gentile	gesso
generality	gentle	gesticulate
generalization	gentility	gesture
generalize	gentleman	geyser
generally	gentlemen	ghastly
generalship	gentleness	ghost
generate	gently	ghostly
generated	gentry	giant
generates	genuflect	gift
generation	genuflection	gifted
generative	genuine	gigantic
generator	genuineness	gild
progenitor	genus	gilded
regenerate	geodetic	gilder
generic	geography	gill
generous	geology	gimlet
generosity	geometry	ginger
genesis	germ	giraffe
genial	germicide	gird
congenial	germinal	girder
geniality	germinate	girdle
genially	germination	girl
genitive	germinative	girlhood

girlish	glide	gluttonous
girth	glided	gnarled
give	glider	gnat
forgive	glimpse	gnaw
gave	glissando	gneiss
given	glisten	gnome
giver	glistened	gnomon
glacier	globe	gnu
glacial	globular	go
glad	globule	gocart
gladden	gloom	gone
gladdened	gloomily	goat
gladly	gloominess	gobble
gladness	glory	goblet
gladsome	glories	God
gladiator	glorification	godchild
gladiatorial	glorify	goddess
gladiolus	glorious	godfather
glamour	inglorious	godhead
glamorous	glossary	godhood
glass	glossiness	godless
glassful	glove	godlike
glassiness	glucose	godling
glazier	glue	godly
gleeful	glutton	godparent

godsend	gossip	graduation
goggle	gouache	undergraduate
goiter	gouge	grain
gold	gourd	granary
golden	govern	grammar
goldenrod	governable	grammarian
goldfish	governess	grammatical
goldsmith	government	grand
golf	governmental	aggrandize
golfer	governor	grandchild
gondola	misgovern	grandeur
gondolier	ungovernable	grandfather
good	grace	grandiloquence
good-by	graceful	grandiloquent
goodliness	graceless	grandiose
goodly	gracious	grandly
goodness	grade	grandness
goose	degrade	grandparent
gooseberry	gradation	granite
gopher	gradient	grant
gorge	ungraded	granulate
gorgeous	gradual	granule
gorilla	gradually	grape
gospel	graduate	grapefruit
gossamer	graduated	grapeshot

grapevine	greasiness	grimy
graphic	great	grind
graphical	greater	grinder
graphics	greatest	grindstone
graphophone	greatly	groaned
grapple	greatness	grocer
grasshopper	greed	grocery
grateful	greedier	groom
gratification	greediest	groomed
gratify	greedily	grotesque
gratis	greediness	ground
gratitude	green	background
gratuitous	greener	foreground
gratuity	greenery	groundless
ingrate	greenhorn	groundwork
ingratitude	greenhouse	underground
ungrateful	greenish	group
gravamen	greenroom	grovel
gravel	gregarious	grow
gravitate	Gregorian	grower
gravitation	gridiron	grown
gravity	grief	growl
grease	grievance	grub
greasewood	grievous	grudge
greasily	grimace	gruel

gruesome	beguile	gunpowder
gruff	guillotine	gunshot
grumble	guilt	gunsmith
grunt	guiltily	gunstock
guarantee	guiltiness	gunwale
guaranteed	guiltless	gurgle
guarantor	guilty	gush
guard	guinea	gusher
guarded	guise	gusset
guardian	guitar	gust
guardsman	gullet	gusto
guava	gullible	gutter
gubernatorial	gulp	guttural
gucrdon	gum	gymnasium
guerrilla	gun	gymnast
guide	gunboat	gymnastic
guidance	guncotton	gypsum
guidebook	gunfire	gypsy
guided	gunman	gyrate
guild	gunner	gyratory
guile	gunnery	gyroscope

H

haberdasher	halberd	handspring
haberdashery	halibut	handwriting
habit	Halloween	longhand
habitable	hallucination	shorthand
habitant	hallucinatory	handle
habitat	halogen	handlebar
habitation	halter	handsome
habitual	hammer	hang
habituate	hammerless	hanger
habituated	hammock	hangman
habitude	hamper	hanker
habitué	hampered	hansom
hackman	unhampered	haphazard
hackneyed	hand	hapless
hacksaw	handball	happen
haddock	handbook	happened
haggle	handcuff	happy
hailstone	handful	happily
hair	handicap	happiness
hairbreadth	handicraft	unhappy
hairbrush	handily	harangue
hairdresser	handiness	harass
hairpin	handiwork	harbinger
hairspring	handkerchief	harbor
	handmade	hard

harden	harmonize	hatchet
hardened	harness	hatchway
hardener	harp	hate
hard-fisted	harpist	hated
hard-headed	harpoon	hateful
hard-hearted	harpsichord	hatefully
hardihood	harrier	hatefulness
hardiness	harsh	hatred
hardness	harsher	haughty
hardpan	harshest	haul
hard-shell	harshly	haulage
hardship	harshness	hauled
hardware	hartshorn	haunt
unhardened	harvest	haunted
harelip	harvester	have
Harlequin	harvests	havoc
harm	hash	hawk
harmful	hassock	hawker
harmless	haste	hawk-eyed
unharmed	hasten	hawkweed
harmony	hastened	hay
harmonic	hastily	haycock
harmonica	hastiness	hayloft
harmonious	hatch	haymow
harmonization	hatchery	hayrack

hayseed	headsman	heartbeat
haystack	headstone	heartbreak
hazard	headstrong	heartbroken
haphazard	headwater	heartburn
hazardous	headway	heartened
haze	headwork	heartfelt
hazily	heal	heartily
haziness	healed	heartless
hazel	healer	heart-rending
head	health	hearth
headache	healthful	hearthstone
headband	healthfulness	heater
headboard	healthily	heath
headdress	unhealed	heathen
headed	unhealthy	heathenish
headfirst	hear	heathenism
headgear	heard	heather
headily	hearer	heaven
headland	hearsay	heavenly
headless	unheard	heavenward
headlight	hearken	heavy
headline	hearse	heavier
headlong	heart	heaviest
headpiece	downhearted	heavily
headquarters	heartache	heaviness

hecatomb	helix	herald
heckle	heliograph	heraldic
hectic	heliotrope	heraldry
hectograph	helium	herb
hedge	help	herbaceous
hedgehog	helped	herbage
hedgerow	helper	herbal
hedonism	helpfully	herbarium
heed	helpfulness	herbivorous
heeded	helpless	Herculean
heedfully	helpmate	here
heedfulness	hematite	hereabouts
heedless	hemicycle	hereafter
heedlessness	hemisphere	hereat
hegemony	hemlock	hereby
hegira	hemorrhage	hereinafter
heifer	hemstitch	hereinbefore
height	hence	hereof
heighten	henceforth	hereto
heinous	henceforward	heretofore
heir	henequen	hereunto
heiress	hepatica	hereupon
heirloom	heptagon	herewith
helical	heptameter	heredity
helicoid	heptangular	hereditability

hereditable	unhesitating	highlander
hereditament	heterogeneous	highly
hereditary	heterogeneity	high-minded
heritability	homogeneous	highness
heritable	hexagon	high-pressure
heritage	hexagonal	highroad
inherit	hexameter	highway
heresy	hexangular	highwayman
heretic	hexapod	hike
hermetic	hiatus	hilarious
hermit	hibernate	hilarity
hermitage	hibernation	hill
hero	hickory	hilliness
heroic	hide	hillock
heroical	hidden	hillside
heroine	hideous	hilltop
heroism	hierarchy	hilt
heron	hieratic	himself
herring	high	hinder
herself	height	hindrance
hesitate	heighten	hinge
hesitance	highborn	hint
hesitancy	highboy	hinted
hesitant	high-handed	hippodrome
hesitation	highland	hippopotamus

hire		hollow		homonym	
hireling		holy		homunculus	
hirsute		holily		honest	
his		holiness		dishonest	
hiss		unholy		honestly	
histology		homage		honesty	
history		home		honey	
historian		homeless		honeybee	
historic		homelike		honeycomb	
historical		homeliness		honeyed	
histrionic		homesickness		honeymoon	
hitch		homespun		honeysuckle	
hither		homestead		honor	
hitherto		homeward		dishonor	
hive		homeopathy		honorable	
hoard		Homeric		honorarium	
hobble		homicide		honorary	
hog		homicidal		unhonored	
hogback		homily		hood	
hogfish		homiletics		hooded	
hoggish		hominy		hoodwink	
hogshead		homogeneous		hookworm	
hogweed		heterogeneous		hope	
hoist		homogeneity		hopefully	
holiday		homologous		hopefulness	

hopelessly	horsewoman	houses
unhoped	unhorsed	housewarming
hopscotch	hortatory	housewife
horizon	horticulture	housework
horizontal	hosier	ice house
horizontally	hosiery	storehouse
horned	hospital	warehouse
hornet	hospitality	hovel
horoscope	hostage	hover
horror	hostile	how
horrible	hostilely	anyhow
horrid	hostility	however
horrify	hot	howsoever
horse	hot-headed	somehow
horseback	hothouse	howitzer
horse-chestnut	hotness	hubbub
horseflesh	hound	huckleberry
horsefly	hour	huckster
horsehair	hourglass	huge
horsehide	hourly	Huguenot
horseman	house	hulk
horsepower	household	human
horse-radish	householder	humane
horseshoe	housekeeper	humaneness
horsewhip	housemaid	humanism

humanitarian		hundredth		huskiness	
humanity		hunger		hussar	
humanization		hungered		hustings	
humanize		hungrily		hustle	
humankind		hunk		hustled	
humble		hunt		hustler	
humbleness		hunted		hutch	
humblest		hunter		hyacinth	
humbug		huntsman		hyaline	
humdrum		hurdle		hybrid	
humid		hurdled		hydrant	
humidify		hurdler		hydrate	
humidity		hurl		hydraulic	
humidor		hurricane		hydrocarbon	
humiliate		hurry		hydrochloric	
humiliation		unhurried		hydroelectric	
humility		hurt		hydrogen	
hummock		hurtful		hydrometer	
humor		hurtfulness		hydrophobia	
humorist		unhurt		hydroplane	
humorous		husband		hydrostatics	
humorousness		husbandry		hydroxide	
hunch		husbands		hygiene	
hundred		husk		hygienic	
hundredfold		huskily		hygienically	

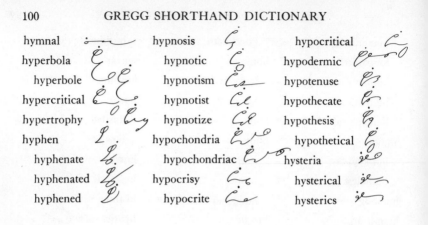

hymnal	hypnosis	hypocritical
hyperbola	hypnotic	hypodermic
hyperbole	hypnotism	hypotenuse
hypercritical	hypnotist	hypothecate
hypertrophy	hypnotize	hypothesis
hyphen	hypochondria	hypothetical
hyphenate	hypochondriac	hysteria
hyphenated	hypocrisy	hysterical
hyphened	hypocrite	hysterics

I

iambic
ibex
ibis
ice
  iceberg
  icebound
  ice house
  iceman
  icicle
  icily
  iciness
ichor
ichthyology
icon
  iconoclasm
  iconoclast
idea
  ideas
ideal
  idealism
  idealist
  idealistic
  ideality
  idealization

idealize
ideally
identic
identical
identification
identify
identity
  unidentified
idiocy
idiot
idiotic
idiom
  idiomatic
  unidiomatic
idiosyncrasy
idle
idled
idleness
idler
idly
idol
idolater
idolatry
idolize
idyl

idyllic
igneous
ignite
  ignites
  ignition
ignoble
ignominy
  ignominious
ignorance
  ignorant
  ignorantly
ignore
iguana
ilk
illegal
  illegality
illegible
illegitimate
illiberal
illicit
illiterate
  illiteracy
illness
illogical
illuminate

illuminant	imitate	immobilization
illumination	imitable	immobilize
illuminator	imitation	immoderate
illumine	imitative	immodest
illusion	imitator	immolate
illusive	inimitable	immoral
illusory	immaculate	immorality
illustrate	immaculately	immortal
illustration	immanent	immortality
illustrative	immaterial	immortalize
illustrator	immature	immortally
illustrious	immeasurable	immovable
image	immediate	immune
imagery	immediately	immunity
imagine	immediateness	immunize
imaginable	immemorial	immunology
imaginary	immense	immure
imagination	immensely	immutable
imaginative	immerse	immutability
unimaginable	immersion	imp
imbecile	immigrant	impish
imbecility	immigration	impact
imbibe	imminent	impair
imbroglio	imminence	impaired
imbue	immobile	impairment

unimpaired	impedance	impersonate
impale	impediment	impersonation
impalpable	impedimenta	impersonator
impalpability	impel	impertinent
impanel	impend	impertinence
impart	impenetrable	imperturbable
impartial	impenetrability	imperturbability
impartiality	impenitent	impervious
impartially	impenitence	impetuous
impassion	imperative	impetuosity
impassionate	imperceptible	impetus
impassioned	imperfect	impinge
impassive	imperfection	impious
impassivity	imperfectly	impiety
impatient	imperforate	implacable
impatience	imperial	implacability
impeach	imperialism	implant
impeachable	imperialist	implement
impeachment	imperialistic	implicate
unimpeachable	imperially	implication
impeccable	imperious	implicit
impeccability	imperil	implore
impecunious	imperiled	imply
impecuniosity	imperishable	implied
impede	impersonal	impolite

impolitely	impracticable	improper
impolitic	impracticability	impropriety
imponderable	imprecate	improve
import	imprecation	improvable
importable	imprecatory	improvement
importance	impregnable	uninproved
important	impregnability	improvident
importation	impregnate	improvise
imported	impregnation	improvisation
importer	impresario	imprudent
unimportant	imprescriptible	imprudence
importune	impress	impudent
importunacy	impression	impudence
importunate	impressionable	impugn
importunity	impressionism	impugnable
impose	impressionistic	impugned
imposition	impressive	impugnment
impossible	imprimatur	impulse
impossibility	imprint	impulsion
impost	imprison	impulsive
impostor	imprisoned	impunity
imposture	imprisonment	impure
impotent	improbable	impurely
impoverish	improbability	impurity
impoverishment	impromptu	impute

imputable	inappreciable	incapacitation
imputation	inappreciative	incarcerate
imputative	inappropriate	incarnate
inability	inapt	incarnation
unable	inaptitude	incendiary
inaccessible	inarticulate	incense
inaccessibility	inartistic	incentive
inaccurate	inasmuch	inception
inaccuracy	inattention	incertitude
inaction	attention	incessant
inactive	attentive	inch
inactivity	inattentive	inchoate
inadequate	inaudible	incident
inadequacy	inaugurate	incidence
inadmissible	inaugural	incidental
inadvertent	inauguration	incidentally
inadvisable	inauspicious	incinerate
inadvisability	inborn	incineration
inalienable	incalculable	incinerator
inane	incandesce	incipient
inanity	incandescence	incise
inanimate	incandescent	incised
inanition	incantation	incision
inapplicable	incapable	incisive
inapposite	incapacitate	incisor

incite	incompatibility	incorrect
incitement	incompetent	incorrigible
incivility	incompetence	incorrigibility
inclement	incomplete	incorruptible
clement	incomprehensible	incorruptibility
inclemency	incomprehensibility	increase
incline	inconclusive	increased
decline	incongruous	incredible
inclination	incongruity	incredibility
inclined	inconsequential	incredulity
recline	inconsiderate	incredulous
inclose	inconsiderable	increment
inclosure	inconsistent	incriminate
include	inconsistency	incrimination
included	inconsolable	incriminatory
inclusion	inconspicuous	incubate
inclusive	inconspicuously	incubation
incognito	inconstancy	incubator
incoherent	incontestable	incubus
incoherence	incontrovertible	inculcate
incombustible	inconvenient	inculcation
income	inconvenience	inculpate
incommensurate	incorporate	inculpation
incomparable	incorporation	inculpatory
incompatible	incorporator	incumbent

incunabula	indented	indifferent
incur	indention	indifferently
incurable	indenture	indigenous
indebtedness	independent	indigent
indecent	independence	indigence
indecency	indescribable	indigestion
indecision	indestructible	indigestible
indecisive	indeterminate	indignant
indecorous	indeterminable	indignation
indecorum	index	indignity
indeed	indexer	indigo
indefatigable	indexes	indirect
indefensible	indices	indirection
indefinable	Indian	indirectness
indefinite	indicate	indiscreet
indefiniteness	contraindicate	indiscretion
indelible	indication	indiscriminate
indelibility	indicative	indispensable
indelicate	indicator	indispose
indelicacy	indicatory	indisposition
indemnify	indicia	indisputable
indemnification	indict	indissoluble
indemnity	indictable	indistinct
indent	indictment	indistinctly
indentation	indifference	indistinctness

indistinguishable	induction	ineligible
indite	inductive	ineluctable
individual	inductor	inept
individualism	indulge	ineptitude
individualist	indulgence	inequality
individualistic	indulgent	inequitable
individuality	industry	ineradicable
individualize	industrial	inerrant
indivisible	industrialism	inert
indolent	industrialist	inertia
indolence	industrialize	inertness
indomitable	industrially	inestimable
indoors	industrious	inevitable
indorse	inebriate	inevitability
indorsed	inebriation	inexact
indorsee	inebriety	inexactitude
indorsement	inedible	inexcusable
indorser	ineffable	inexhaustible
indorses	ineffective	inexhaustibility
unindorsed	ineffectual	inexhaustibly
indubitable	ineffectually	inexorable
induce	inefficient	inexpedient
inducement	inefficiency	inexpensive
induct	inelegance	inexperience
inductance	inelegant	inexplicable

inextricable	infernal	inflection
inextricability	inferno	inflexible
infallible	infertile	inflexibility
infallibility	infertility	inflict
infamy	infest	infliction
infamous	infidel	influence
infant	infidelity	influential
infancy	infiltrate	uninfluenced
infanticide	infinite	influenza
infantile	infinitesimal	influx
infantry	infinitive	efflux
infatuate	infinitude	inform
infatuated	infinity	informal
infatuation	infirm	informality
infeasible	infirmary	informant
infect	infirmity	information
infection	inflame	informative
infectious	inflammability	informer
infelicitous	inflammable	misinform
infelicity	inflammation	uninformed
infer	inflammatory	infraction
inference	inflate	infrangible
inferential	inflated	infrequent
inferior	inflation	infringe
inferiority	inflect	infringement

infuriate	inhabited	inhumanity
infuriated	uninhabited	inimical
infuse	inhale	inimitable
infusible	inhalation	iniquity
infusion	inhaled	iniquitous
ingenious	inhaler	initial
ingenuity	inharmonious	initially
ingenuous	inhere	initiate
ingest	inhered	initiation
ingestion	inherence	initiatory
inglorious	inherent	uninitiated
ingot	inherit	inject
ingrain	disinherit	injection
ingrained	hereditary	injector
ingratiate	heritage	injudicious
ingratiation	inheritable	injunction
ingratiatory	inheritance	injure
ingredient	inherited	injured
ingress	inheritor	injuries
ingrown	inhibit	injurious
inhabit	inhibition	injury
inhabitable	inhibitory	uninjured
inhabitancy	inhospitable	injustice
inhabitant	inhuman	unjust
inhabitation	inhumane	ink

inkhorn	innumerable	inscriber
inkling	inoculate	inscription
inkstand	inoffensive	inscrutable
inkwell	inoperable	inscrutability
inky	inoperative	insect
inlaid	inopportune	insecticide
inland	inopportuneness	insectivorous
inlet	inordinate	insecure
inmate	coordinate	insecurity
inmost	subordinate	insensible
inn	inorganic	insensate
innate	inpatient	insensibility
inner	inquest	insensitive
innermost	inquietude	insentience
inning	inquire	insentient
innocence	inquirer	inseparable
innocent	inquires	insert
innocently	inquiries	inserted
innocents	inquiry	insertion
innocuous	inquisition	inset
innovate	inquisitive	inshore
innovation	insane	inside
innovative	insanity	insider
innovator	insanitary	insidious
innuendo	inscribe	insight

insignia	inspire	institutional
insignificant	inspiration	instruct
insignificance	inspirational	instruction
insincere	inspired	instructional
insincerely	inspirer	instructive
insincerity	inspires	instructor
insinuate	instability	instructress
insinuated	install	uninstructed
insinuation	installation	instrument
insipid	installed	instrumental
insipidity	installment	instrumentalist
insist	instant	instrumentality
insistence	instance	instrumentally
insistent	instantaneous	instrumentation
insobriety	instantly	insubordinate
insolent	instead	insubordination
insolence	instep	insufferable
insoluble	instigate	insufficient
insolvency	instigation	insulate
insolvent	instigator	insular
insomnia	instill	insularity
insomuch	instinct	insulation
inspect	instinctive	insulator
inspection	institute	uninsulated
inspector	institution	insult

insults	integument	intentness
insuperable	intellect	unintentional
insuperability	intellectual	interborough
insupportable	intellectually	intercede
insuppressible	intelligent	interceded
insure	intelligence	intercession
insurability	intelligibility	intercept
insurable	intelligible	interception
insurance	unintelligent	interchangeable
uninsured	intemperate	intercollegiate
insurgent	intemperance	intercourse
insurmountable	intemperately	interdenom-inational
insurrection	intend	interdependent
insurrectionary	intent	interdict
intact	intention	interdiction
intaglio	intendant	interest
intake	intense	interested
intangible	intensification	uninterested
intangibility	intensify	interfere
integer	intensity	interference
disintegrate	intensive	interim
integral	intent	interior
integrate	intend	interject
integration	intention	interlock
integrity	intentional	interlocutor

interloper	interpret	intervention
interlude	interpretation	non-intervention
intermarriage	interpretative	interview
intermediate	interpreter	interweave
intermediary	interregnum	intestate
intermezzo	interrelation	intestine
interminable	interrogate	intimate
intermingle	interrogation	intimacy
intermit	interrogative	intimated
intermission	interrogatory	intimation
intermittence	interrupt	intimidate
intermittent	interrupted	intimidated
intermixture	interruption	intimidation
intern	uninterrupted	into
internment	interscholastic	intolerance
internal	intersect	intolerable
internally	intersperse	intolerant
international	interstate	intone
internecine	interstice	intonation
interpellate	interstices	intoxicate
interpellation	interstitial	intoxicant
interpolate	intertwine	intoxicated
interpolation	intertwined	intoxication
interpose	interval	non-intoxicating
interposition	intervene	intractable

intransigent	intrusive	inventory
intransigence	intrust	inverse
intransitive	intuition	inversion
intrastate	intuitive	invert
intrenchment	inunction	inverted
intrepid	inundate	invest
intrepidity	inundation	invested
intricate	inure	investment
extricate	invade	investor
intricacy	invasion	invests
intrigue	invalid	reinvest
intrinsic	invalidate	investigate
extrinsic	invalidation	investigation
introduce	invalidity	investigative
introduction	invaluable	investigator
introductory	invar	inveterate
introit	invariable	invidious
introspect	invariability	invigorate
introspection	inveigh	invigoration
introspective	invective	invincible
introvert	inveigle	invincibility
introversion	invent	inviolable
intrude	invention	inviolability
intruder	inventive	inviolate
intrusion	inventor	invisible

invisibility	ionize	irrationally
invite	Ionic	irreclaimable
invitation	iota	irreconcilable
uninvited	ipecac	irrecoverable
invoice	irate	irredeemable
invoices	irascibility	irrefragable
invoke	irascible	irrefrangible
invocation	iris	irrefutable
involuntary	iridescence	irregular
involuntarily	iridescent	irregularity
involute	iridium	irrelevant
involution	irk	irreligious
involve	irksome	irremediable
invulnerable	iron	irremovable
invulnerability	flatiron	irreparable
inward	ironclad	irreplaceable
inwardly	ironside	irrepressible
inwardness	ironware	irreproachable
iodine	ironwood	irresistible
iodate	ironwork	irresistibility
iodic	irony	irresoluble
iodide	ironical	irresolute
iodize	irradiate	irresolution
ion	irradiation	irrespective
ionization	irrational	irresponsible

irresponsibility	irritative	isthmus
irretraceable	irruption	Italy
irretrievable	isinglass	Italian
irreverent	Islam	itchy
irreverence	island	item
irreversible	isobar	itemize
irrevocable	isolate	itinerate
irrigate	isolation	itinerancy
irrigation	isomeric	itinerant
irritate	isotherm	itinerary
irritability	issue	its
irritable	issuance	itself
irritant	reissue	ivory
irritation	unissued	ivy

J

jackal	jewelry	jollity
Jacobean	Jewish	jonquil
jaguar	jingle	jostle
janitor	jingo	jot
January	jingoism	jounce
japan	jinrikisha	journal
jargon	jinx	journalism
jasmine	jitney	journalist
jaundice	jockey	journalize
jauntily	jocose	journey
jealous	jocosity	jovial
Jehovah	jocular	joviality
jejune	jocularity	jowl
jellyfish	jocund	joy
jeopardy	jocundity	enjoy
jeopardize	join	joyful
jerk	adjoin	joyless
jerkily	disjoin	joyous
jersey	enjoin	jubilate
Jesus	jointed	jubilance
Jesuit	jointure	jubilant
jetsam	joist	jubilation
jettison	joker	jubilee
jewel	jolly	judge
	jollification	adjudge

judged	junction	injustice
judgeship	juncture	justice
judgment	jungle	justiciar
judicial	junior	justifiable
judicative	juniper	justification
judicatory	junk	justificatory
judicature	jurist	justify
judicially	juridical	justly
judiciary	jurisdiction	justness
judicious	jurisprudence	unjust
juggle	juror	unjustifiable
jugular	jury	juvenile
jumble	juryman	juvenility
jump	just	juxtaposition

K

kaiser	kind	kith
kaleidoscope	kinder	kitten
kaleidoscopic	kindest	kleptomaniac
kangaroo	kindliness	knave
kaolin	kindly	knavery
keep	kindness	knavish
bookkeeper	kinds	kneecap
housekeeper	unkind	knight
keeper	kindergarten	knighted
keepsake	kindred	knights
kept	kine	unknightly
timekeeper	kinetic	knot
kennel	king	knotted
kernel	kingbird	unknotted
kerosene	kingbolt	know
kersey	kingcraft	knew
keyboard	kingdom	knowable
khedive	kingfisher	knowingness
kidnap	kinglet	knowledge
kidney	kingliness	known
kiln	king-pin	unknown
kilogram	kingship	knuckle
kilometer	kinsman	knurl
kilt	kiosk	kopeck
	kitchen	krypton

L

label	ladylike	landholder
labial	ladyship	landlady
labor	laggard	landlocked
laboratory	lagoon	landlord
labored	laity	landmark
laborer	lambent	landowner
laborious	lame	landscape
laburnum	lamed	landslip
labyrinth	lamely	landsman
lacerate	lameness	landward
lacerated	lament	language
laceration	lamentable	languid
lachrymal	lamentation	languish
lachrymose	lamented	languor
lacquer	lamina	languorous
lacrosse	laminate	lantern
lactic	laminated	lanthanum
lacuna	lamination	lanyard
lacunae	lampoon	lapel
lacunas	lamprey	lapidary
ladder	lancet	lapse
laden	lancination	larboard
ladle	land	larceny
lady	landed	larcenous
	landfall	larch

lard	later	laugh
large	latest	laughable
enlarge	latter	laughingstock
largely	latent	laughter
larger	lateral	launch
largest	laterally	launder
lariat	lath	laundress
lark	lathe	laundry
larkspur	lather	laundryman
larva	Latin	laurel
larval	Latinism	laureate
larynx	Latinist	lava
laryngitis	Latinity	lavaliere
lassitude	latitude	lavatory
lasso	latitudinal	lavender
last	latter	lavish
lasted	lattermost	law
lastly	lattice	lawful
lasts	latticework	lawgiver
latch	laud	lawless
latchkey	laudability	lawmaker
latchstring	laudable	lawsuit
late	laudation	lawyer
lately	laudatory	lax
lateness	laudanum	laxative

laxity	leather	legation
laxness	leatheret	legato
relax	leathern	legend
layer	leatheroid	legendary
lazy	leatherwood	legerdemain
lazily	leathery	legging
laziness	leaven	legible
lead	lectern	illegible
leaden	lecture	legibility
leader	lecturer	legion
leadership	ledger	legionary
leadsman	leeward	legislate
league	leeway	legislation
leak	left	legislative
leakage	left-handed	legislator
leakiness	legacy	legislature
learn	legal	legitimate
learned	illegal	illegitimate
learnt	legalism	legitimacy
lease	legality	legitimateness
leasehold	legalization	legitimation
leaseholder	legalize	legitimatize
lessee	legally	legitimist
lessor	legate	legume
least	legatee	leguminous

leisure	
leisureliness	
leisurely	
lemon	
lemonade	
lemur	
length	
lengthen	
lengthily	
lengthiness	
lengthways	
lengthwise	
lengthy	
lenient	
lenience	
leniently	
lenitive	
lenity	
Lent	
Lenten	
lentil	
lenticular	
leonine	
leopard	
leper	

leprosy	
leprous	
lesion	
less	
least	
lessen	
lessened	
lesser	
lesson	
let	
lethal	
lethargy	
lethargic	
lethargical	
letter	
lettered	
letterhead	
letterpress	
lettuce	
levant	
levee	
level	
leveled	
leveler	
lever	

leverage	
leviathan	
levitate	
levitation	
levity	
lexicon	
lexicography	
liable	
liability	
liaison	
liar	
libation	
libel	
libelant	
libeled	
libelee	
libeler	
libelous	
liberal	
illiberal	
liberalism	
liberality	
liberalization	
liberalizer	
liberally	

liberty		lift		lignite	
liberate		ligate		like	
liberated		ligament		dislike	
liberation		ligation		likable	
liberator		ligature		likelihood	
library		light		likely	
librarian		alight		liken	
libretto		delightful		likened	
license		enlightenment		likeness	
licensed		lighted		likes	
licensee		lighten		likewise	
licentiate		lightened		unlikely	
lichen		lighter		lilac	
licorice		lightest		lilt	
lictor		lighthouse		lily	
liege		lightly		limber	
lien		light-minded		lime	
lieu		lightness		limekiln	
lieutenant		lightning		limelight	
life		lights		limewater	
lifeless		lightship		limit	
lifelike		lightsome		limitable	
lifelong		relight		limitation	
lifetime		ligneous		limited	
lives		lignify		limitless	

limousine	linotype	listener
limpid	lintel	liter
limpidity	lion	literate
linden	lioness	illiterate
line	lionize	literacy
align	liquid	literal
lineage	liquefaction	literalism
lineal	liquefiable	literality
lineament	liquefy	literalize
linear	liquescent	literary
lined	liquidate	literature
lineman	liquidation	transliterate
liner	liquidator	litharge
reline	liquidity	lithe
unlined	liquor	lithesome
linen	lira	lithia
linger	lire	lithium
lingerie	lissom	lithograph
lingual	list	litigate
linguist	enlist	litigable
linguistic	listless	litigant
linguistics	lists	litigation
liniment	reenlist	litigious
linkage	listen	litmus
linoleum	listened	litter

little	localism	loftiness
littoral	locality	logarithm
liturgy	localization	loggia
liturgic	localize	logic
live	locally	illogical
live	locate	logical
lived	allocate	logician
livelihood	dislocate	logotype
liveliness	location	logwood
livelong	lock	loiter
liver	locker	loitered
livery	locket	loiterer
livid	lockjaw	lone
lizard	lockout	loneliness
loaf	locksmith	lonesome
loaves	locomotion	lonesomeness
loam	locomotive	long
loathe	locus	belong
loathful	loci	elongate
loathly	locust	longboat
loathsome	lodge	longed
lobby	lodger	longer
lobbyist	lodgment	longest
lobster	loft	longevity
local	loftily	longhand

longhorn	lotus	low-spirited
longitude	loud	loyal
longitudinal	louder	loyalist
longshoreman	loudest	loyalty
prolong	loudly	lubricate
look	loudness	lubricant
outlook	lounge	lubrication
loop	love	lubricator
loophole	lovable	lucent
loose	loveless	lucid
loosen	loveliness	lucidity
loosened	lovely	luck
looseness	lover	luckily
loquacious	lovesick	luckiness
loquacity	unlovable	luckless
lord	low	lucrative
lordliness	lowborn	lucubration
lordship	lowboy	ludicrous
lore	lower	luggage
lorgnette	lowermost	lugubrious
lose	lowest	lukewarm
losable	lowland	lumbago
loss	lowliness	lumber
lost	lowness	luminous
lottery	low-pressure	luminary

luminescent	lurid	luxuriate
luminosity	lurk	luxurious
lump	luscious	lyceum
lunar	luster	lymphatic
lunacy	lustrous	lynx
lunatic	lute	lyonnaise
lunch	Lutheran	lyre
luncheon	luxury	lyric
lurch	luxuriance	lyrical
lure	luxuriant	lyricism

M

macabre	madrigal	magnificence
macadam	magazine	magnifico
macadamize	magenta	magnify
macaroni	maggot	magnification
macaroon	Magi	magnifier
macerate	magic	magniloquent
maceration	magician	magnitude
machete	magistrate	magnolia
machicolation	magisterial	magpie
machination	magistracy	maharaja
machine	magistral	mahogany
machinery	magistrature	maid
machinist	magnanimous	maiden
mackerel	magnanimity	maidenhair
macrocosm	magnate	maidenhood
microcosm	magnesium	maidenly
macron	magnesia	mail
maculate	magnet	mailable
immaculate	magnetic	mailed
mad	magnetically	mailer
madhouse	magnetism	unmailable
madman	magnetization	maim
madness	magnetize	maimed
madam	magneto	main
	magnificent	mainland

mainly	malapropos	malnutrition
mainmast	malaria	malodorous
mainsail	malarial	malpractice
mainspring	malassimilation	malt
mainstay	malcontent	Maltese
maintain	male	maltreat
maintainable	female	malversation
maintained	malediction	mammoth
maintenance	maledictory	man
majesty	malefactor	manhole
majestic	maleficent	manhood
majolica	malevolent	mankind
major	malfeasance	manly
majority	malformation	manslaughter
make	malice	men
make-believe	malicious	unmanned
maker	malign	manacle
makeshift	malignancy	manage
make-up	malignant	manageability
unmake	malignity	manageable
maladjustment	malignly	management
maladministration	malinger	manager
maladroit	malingerer	managerial
malady	malleable	managerially
malapert	malleability	managership

unmanageable	manner	marconigram
manatee	mannerism	mare
mandamus	mannerless	margin
mandarin	mannerly	marginal
mandate	unmannerly	marginalia
mandatory	manor	marginally
mandible	manorial	margrave
mandolin	mansion	marigold
maneuver	mantelpiece	marine
manganese	manual	mariner
manger	manually	submarine
mangy	manufacture	ultramarine
mania	manufactory	marionette
maniac	manufacturer	marital
maniacal	manumission	maritime
manicure	manure	mark
manicurist	manuscript	marked
manifest	many	markedly
manifestation	maple	marker
manifestly	maraschino	marksman
manifesto	maraud	unmarked
manifold	marauder	market
manifolder	marble	marketability
manikin	march	marketable
manipulate	marcher	marmalade

marmoset	masterful	materialization
maroon	masterliness	materialize
marooned	masterly	materially
marquis	masterpiece	maternal
marquise	masters	maternally
marry	mastership	maternity
marriage	masterwork	mathematics
marriageable	mastery	mathematician
unmarried	masthead	matinée
marshal	masticate	matricide
martial	mastication	matriculate
martially	mastiff	matrimony
martyr	mastodon	matrimonial
martyrdom	matador	matrimonially
marvel	match	matrix
marvelous	matchless	matrices
mascot	matchmaker	matron
masculine	matchwood	matter
masculinity	unmatched	mattress
mason	material	mature
masonry	immaterial	immature
massacre	materialism	maturity
massage	materialist	premature
massive	materialistic	maudlin
master	materiality	mausoleum

mauve	mechanical	meditate
maverick	mechanician	meditation
maxim	mechanism	meditative
maximum	mechanization	medium
mayhem	mechanize	media
mayonnaise	medal	mediums
mayor	medalist	meerschaum
mazurka	medallion	melancholy
meager	meddlesome	melancholia
mean	median	melancholic
meanly	mediate	meliorate
meanness	mediation	ameliorate
meantime	mediative	melioration
meanwhile	mediator	mellifluous
meander	medical	melodrama
measles	medicament	melodramatic
measure	medicate	melody
commensurate	medication	melodeon
measurably	medicative	melodic
measured	medicinal	melodious
measureless	medicine	melt
measurement	medieval	member
measurer	medievally	membership
measures	mediocre	memorandum
mechanic	mediocrity	memoranda

memorandums	mentality	meringue
memory	mentally	merino
commemorate	mention	merit
memento	mentioned	merited
memoir	mentor	meritorious
memorabilia	mephitic	unmerited
memorable	mercantile	mermaid
memorial	mercenary	merry
memorization	mercerize	merrily
memorize	merchant	merriment
menace	merchandise	merrymaking
menage	merchantman	mesa
menagerie	mercury	mesmerize
mendacious	mercurial	mesmerism
mendacity	mercy	mesquite
mendicant	merciful	message
mendicancy	merciless	messenger
menial	mere	metabolism
meningitis	merely	metal
meniscus	merest	metallic
mensuration	meretricious	metalloid
commensurate	merge	metallurgy
dimension	merger	metamorphose
mensurative	meridian	metamorphosis
mental	meridional	metaphor

metaphorical

metaphysics

metaphysical

metaphysician

meteor

meteoric

meteorite

meteorology

meter

method

methodical

methodist

meticulous

metric

metrical

metronome

metropolis

metropolitan

mezzanine

miasma

miasmal

miasmatic

microbe

microbiology

microcosm

macrocosm

micrometer

microorganism

microphone

microscope

microscopic

midnight

midst

midwinter

might

almighty

mightily

mightiness

mighty

migrate

migration

migratory

mild

mildly

mildness

mildew

mile

mileage

milepost

milestone

militant

militancy

militarism

militarist

militaristic

military

militate

militia

milk

milkman

milkweed

millennium

millenary

millenial

milliner

millinery

million

millionaire

millionth

mimeograph

mimic

mimicry

minaret

minatory

mind

mindful	miracle	miscellany
remind	miraculous	mischief
unmindful	mirage	mischievous
mined	mirror	misconception
mineral	mirth	misconduct
mineralogy	mirthful	misconstrue
mingle	mirthless	misconstruction
miniature	misadventure	miscount
minimize	misalliance	miscounted
minimization	misanthrope	miscreant
minimum	misanthropic	misdeed
minister	misanthropical	misdemeanor
administer	misapprehended	miser
ministerial	misapprehension	misery
ministration	misappropriate	miserable
ministry	misarrange	misfeasance
minor	misbehave	misfire
minster	misbehavior	misfit
minstrel	miscalculate	misfortune
mint	miscarry	misgiving
minuet	miscarries	misgovern
minus	miscegenation	mishap
minute	miscellaneous	misinform
minute	miscellanea	misinterpret
minutia	miscellanist	misjudged

misleading	mistook	moaned
mislike	mistreat	mobile
mismanage	mistress	immobile
misname	mistrial	mobility
misnomer	mistrust	mobilization
misplace	distrust	mobilize
misprint	mistrustful	moccasin
mispronounce	misunderstand	mock
misquote	misunderstood	mockery
misread	misuse	moderate
misrepresent	miter	immoderate
misrepresentation	mitered	moderately
misrule	mitigate	moderateness
missile	mitigable	moderation
mission	mitigation	moderator
missionary	mitten	modern
missive	mix	modernism
misspell	admixture	modernist
misspelled	miscible	modernity
misstate	mixed	modernization
misstatement	mixer	modernize
mistake	mixes	modest
mistakenly	mixture	modestly
unmistakable	mnemonic	modesty
mistletoe	moan	modicum

modify	momentarily	monogamous
modification	momentary	monogram
modifier	momently	monograph
modulate	momentous	monolith
mohair	momentum	monologue
Mohammedan	monarch	monologist
moist	anarchy	monomania
moisten	monarchial	monoplane
moistened	monarchism	monopoly
moistly	monarchist	monopolism
moisture	monarchy	monopolist
molasses	monastery	monopolistic
mold	monastic	monopolization
molecule	money	monopolize
molecular	monetary	monotone
molehill	monetize	monotonous
molest	moneyed	monotony
molestation	mongoose	monotype
unmolested	mongrel	monsoon
mollify	monitor	monster
mollification	monk	monstrosity
mollusk	monkey	monstrous
molten	monocle	month
molybdenum	monody	monthly
moment	monogamy	monument

monumental	furthermore	almost
mood	moreover	inmost
moodily	moribund	mostly
moodiness	morning	uppermost
moon	morocco	utmost
moonlight	moron	uttermost
moonshine	morose	motet
moonstone	morphine	mother
moral	morphology	godmother
demoralize	morsel	grandmother
immoral	mortal	motherhood
morale	immortalize	mother-in-law
moralism	mortality	motherland
moralist	mortally	motherless
moralistic	mortar	motherliness
morality	mortgage	mother-of-pearl
moralization	mortgagee	stepmother
moralize	mortgagor	motion
morally	mortify	motioned
moratorium	mortification	motionless
morbid	mortuary	motive
morbidity	mosaic	motivate
morbidly	mosquito	motivation
mordant	mossiness	motley
more	most	motor

motored	move	multiplex
motorist	immovable	multiplicand
motorman	movability	multiplication
motto	movable	multiplicative
mound	movement	multiplicity
mount	mover	multiplier
dismount	movie	multitude
mountain	remove	multitudinous
mountaineer	mower	mumble
mountainous	much	mummer
mounted	mucilage	mummery
remount	mucilaginous	mummy
surmount	mucous	mummification
unmounted	mulatto	mummify
mountebank	mulberry	mumps
mourn	mulct	mundane
mourner	mulcted	municipal
mournful	mule	municipality
mouse	multifarious	municipally
mice	multiform	munificent
mouser	multiformity	munificence
mouth	multigraph	munition
mouthed	multimillionaire	mural
mouthful	multiply	immure
mouthpiece	multiple	murder

murdered	musicale	mutilation
murderess	musician	mutilator
murderous	musket	mutiny
muriatic	musketeer	mutineer
murk	musketry	mutinous
murkily	muskmelon	mutton
murkiness	muskrat	mutual
murmur	muslin	mutually
murmurer	mussel	muzzle
murmurous	must	myopia
muscadine	mustache	myriad
muscatel	mustard	myrtle
muscle	muster	myself
muscular	mutate	mystery
muscularity	immutable	mysterious
muscularly	mutability	mystic
musculature	mutable	mystical
muse	mutation	mysticism
museum	mutative	mystification
mush	transmute	mystify
mushroom	mute	myth
music	muteness	mythical
musical	mutilate	mythology

N

nacre	narrate	national
nacreous	narration	nationalism
nainsook	narrative	nationalistic
naïve	narrator	nationality
naïveté	narrow	nationalization
name	narrowed	nationalize
misnamed	narrower	nationally
namable	narrowest	native
nameless	narrowly	nativity
namely	narrow-minded	nature
names	narrowness	natural
namesake	narwhal	naturalism
nickname	nasal	naturalist
surname	nasality	naturalistic
unnamed	nasalize	naturalization
napery	nasally	naturalize
napkin	nascent	naturally
Napoleon	nasty	naturalness
Napoleonic	nastier	preternatural
narcissus	nastiest	supernatural
narcotic	nastily	unnatural
narcosis	nastiness	naughty
narcotism	natation	naughtiest
narcotize	nation	naughtily
	international	naughtiness

nausea	nebula	neediness
nauseate	nebulosity	needless
nauseous	nebulous	nefarious
nautical	necessary	negative
aeronautic	necessaries	negation
nautilus	necessarily	neglect
navigate	necessitate	neglectful
circumnavigate	necessitous	negligence
navigability	necessity	negligent
navigable	unnecessary	negligible
navigation	neck	negotiate
navigator	neckband	negotiability
navy	neckcloth	negotiable
naval	neckerchief	negotiation
near	necklace	negotiator
nearer	necktie	neighbor
nearest	neckwear	neighborhood
nearly	necrology	neighborly
nearness	necropolis	neither
nearsighted	necromancy	Nemesis
neat	nectar	neolithic
neater	need	neon
neatest	needed	neophyte
neatly	needful	nepenthe
neatness	needfully	nephew

nepotism	newer	nightgown
nerve	newest	nightingale
nerveless	newly	nightly
nervous	newness	nightmare
unnerved	newsmonger	nights
nescient	newspaper	nighttime
nestle	renewable	nihilism
nether	New Year's	nihilist
network	next	nihilistic
neural	nibble	nimble
neuralgia	nice	nimbus
neurasthenia	nicely	niter
neurosis	niceness	nitrate
neurotic	nicer	nitric
neuter	nicest	nitrification
neutral	nicety	nitrify
neutrality	nickel	nitrogen
neutralization	nickeliferous	nitrogenous
neutralize	nickelodeon	nitroglycerin
neutrally	nickname	nitrous
never	nicotine	noble
nevermore	niggard	ignoble
nevertheless	night	nobility
new	nightdress	nobleman
newcomer	nightfall	nobler

noblest

nobody

nocturne

nocturnal

noise

noiseless

noisily

noisiness

noisome

nomad

nomadic

nomenclature

misnomer

nominal

nominally

nominate

denominate

nomination

nominee

nonagenarian

nonagon

non-appearance

nonchalant

nonchalance

non-combatant

non-commissioned

noncommittal

non-communicant

non-conductor

non-conformity

non-conformist

nondescript

nonentity

nonesuch

non-existence

non-metallic

nonpareil

non-participating

non-payment

nonplus

non-resident

non-resistant

nonsense

nonsensical

non-subscriber

non-suit

non-union

noon

noonday

noontide

noontime

norm

abnormal

normal

normalcy

normality

normally

subnormal

Norman

north

northeast

northeaster

northeasterly

northeastern

northeastward

northerly

northern

northerner

northernmost

northland

northwest

northwesterly

northwestern

nose

noseband	notorious	nude
nosebleed	notoriety	nudity
nosegay	notwithstanding	nudge
nostril	noun	nugatory
nostrum	pronoun	nugget
not	nourish	nuisance
note	nourishment	null
annotate	novel	nullification
connote	novelette	nullify
denote	novelist	nullity
notability	novelize	numb
notable	novelty	numbness
notarial	novice	number
notary	novitiate	numberless
notation	now	numeral
notebook	nowadays	enumerate
noted	nowhere	innumerable
noteworthy	noxious	numerate
nothing	innoxious	numeration
nothingness	obnoxious	numerator
notice	nozzle	numerical
noticeable	nucleate	numerous
notify	nuclear	numismatics
notification	nucleation	nuncio
notion	nucleus	nunnery

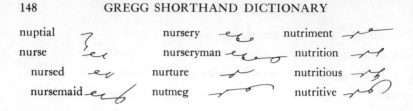

nuptial

nurse

   nursed

   nursemaid

nursery

   nurseryman

nurture

nutmeg

nutriment

nutrition

nutritious

nutritive

O

oat

oaten

oatmeal

oath

obbligato

obdurate

obduracy

obedient

disobedient

obedience

obeisance

obelisk

obese

obesity

obey

disobey

obituary

object

objectify

objection

objectionable

objective

objectivity

objector

unobjectionable

objurgate

oblation

oblige

disoblige

obligate

obligation

obligatory

oblique

obliquity

obliterate

obliteration

transliterate

oblivion

oblivious

oblong

obloquy

obnoxious

oboe

obscene

obscenity

obscure

obscureness

obscurity

obsequious

obsequy

observe

observable

observance

observant

observation

observatory

observer

unobservant

obsess

obsessed

obsession

obsidian

obsolete

obsolescence

obsolescent

obsoletely

obsoleteness

obstacle

obstinate

obstinacy

obstinately

obstreperous

obstruct

obstruction

obstructionist	occlude	octopus
obstructive	occlusion	ocular
obstructor	occult	oculist
unobstructed	occultation	odd
obtain	occultism	oddity
obtainable	occupy	oddness
obtained	occupancy	odium
unobtainable	occupant	odious
obtrude	occupation	odometer
obtruder	occupational	odor
obtrusion	preoccupied	deodorize
obtrusive	unoccupied	malodorous
unobtrusive	occur	odoriferous
obtuse	occurrence	odorless
obverse	ocean	odorous
obviate	oceanic	of
obviation	oceanography	off
obvious	ocher	offal
occasion	ochlocracy	offcast
occasional	octave	off-color
occasionally	octagon	offend
occasioned	octagonal	inoffensive
occident	octameter	offender
occidental	octangular	offense
occiput	octavo	offensive

offer	oldest	onward
office	old-fashioned	thereon
officeholder	oldish	one
officer	oldness	no one
offices	oleomargarine	oneness
official	olfactory	oneself
officially	oligarchy	one-sided
officiate	olive	only
officiation	omega	onomatopoeia
officious	omelet	onus
often	omen	onerous
oftener	ominous	onyx
oftentimes	omit	ooze
ohm	omission	opal
ohmmeter	omnibus	opalesce
oil	omnipotent	opalescence
oilcloth	omnipotence	opalescent
oiler	omnipresent	opaque
oilily	omniscient	opacity
oiliness	nescient	open
oilskin	omniscience	open-air
oilstone	prescient	opener
old	on	open-eyed
olden	onlooker	open-faced
older	onto	open-hearted

open-hearth

openly

openness

openwork

reopen

unopened

opera

operetta

operate

cooperate

operable

operated

operates

operation

operative

operator

ophthalmology

opinion

opinionated

opinionative

opium

opiate

opossum

opponent

opportune

opportunism

opportunist

opportunity

oppose

opposes

opposite

opposition

unopposed

oppress

oppression

oppressive

oppressor

opprobrious

opprobrium

optic

optical

optician

optimism

optimist

optimistic

optimistical

optimum

option

optional

optometry

optometrist

opulent

opulence

opus

opera

or

oracle

oracular

oracularly

oral

orally

orange

orangeade

oration

orator

oratorical

oratorio

oratory

orb

orbit

orchard

orchestra

orchestral

orchestrate

orchestration

orchid	disorganize	ornamental
ordain	organization	ornamentation
ordained	reorganize	ornithology
ordination	unorganized	orotund
ordeal	orgy	orphan
order	orient	orphanage
disorder	oriental	orphaned
orderliness	orientalism	orphanhood
reorder	orientalist	orthochromatic
ordinal	orientate	orthodox
ordinance	orientation	unorthodox
ordinary	orifice	orthoëpy
extraordinary	origin	orthography
ordinarily	original	orthopedic
ordinate	originality	oscillate
coordinate	originally	oscillation
inordinate	originate	oscillator
subordinate	origination	oscillatory
ordnance	originative	osculate
organ	originator	osier
organic	oriole	osmium
organically	Orion	osmosis
organism	ormolu	osprey
organist	ornate	ossify
organize	ornament	osseous

ostentation	outgo	overbalance
ostensible	outgrowth	overboard
ostentatious	outlandish	overburden
osteopath	outlaw	overcapitalize
ostracize	outlet	overcharge
ostracism	outline	overcoat
ostrich	outlined	overcome
other	outlive	overdevelop
otherwise	outlook	overdo
otiose	outnumber	overdraft
otter	output	overdriven
ourselves	outrage	overdue
out	outreach	overexpose
outcast	outrigger	overflow
outclass	outside	overhand
outcome	outstanding	overhang
outcrop	outtalk	overhaul
outcry	outward	overhead
outdistance	outwear	overinfluence
outdoors	outwit	overlap
outer	oval	overlook
outermost	oven	overnight
outfield	over	overpower
outfit	overalls	overproduction
outgeneral	overawe	overreach

overrule	overtone	ownership
overrun	overture	oxalic
overseer	overturn	oxygen
overshadow	overweight	dioxide
overshoe	overwhelm	hydroxide
oversight	overwhelmed	monoxide
oversize	overwrought	oxide
oversubscribe	owl	oxidize
overt	owlet	oxyhydrogen
overtake	owlish	protoxide
overthrow	own	oyster
overtime	owner	ozone

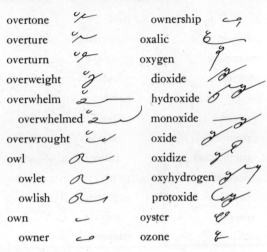

P

pabulum
pacemaker
pachyderm
pacify
  pacific
  pacifically
  pacification
  pacifier
  pacifism
  pacifist
pack
  package
  packer
  packet
pact
pad
paddle
paddock
padlock
pagan
page
  pagination
pageant
  pageantry

paid
  overpaid
  repaid
  unpaid
pain
  painful
  painless
  painstaking
paint
  painted
  painter
pajama
palace
  palatial
palanquin
palate
  palatable
paleography
paleontology
palette
palfrey
palimpsest
palindrome
palisade
pall

palladium
palliate
  palliation
  palliative
pallium
pallor
palmetto
palmist
  palmistry
palpate
  palpability
  palpable
  palpation
  palpitate
palsy
  palsied
paltry
pampas
pamphlet
panacea
panchromatic
  achromatic
orthochromatic
pancreas
  pancreatic

pandemonium	paprika	paranoia
panegyric	par	paranoiac
panegyrical	parity	parapet
panegyrist	parable	paraphernalia
panegyrize	parabola	paraphrase
panel	parabolic	parasite
pang	parabolical	parasitic
panic	parachute	parcel
pannier	parade	parchment
panoply	paradigm	pardon
panorama	paradise	pardonable
panoramic	paradox	unpardonable
pansy	paradoxical	paregoric
pant	paraffin	parent
pantaloon	paragon	parentage
pantheon	paragraph	parental
panther	parallax	parenthesis
pantograph	parallel	parentheses
pantomime	parallelogram	parish
pantry	unparalleled	parishioner
papacy	paralyze	parliament
papal	paralysis	parliamentarian
paper	paralytic	parliamentary
newspaper	paralyzes	unparliamentary
papoose	paramount	parlor

parochial	participate	passion
parody	participant	dispassionate
parole	participle	impassioned
paroxysm	participial	passionate
paroxysmal	particle	passionless
parquet	particular	passive
parricide	particularity	impassive
parricidal	particularize	passivity
parrot	particularly	passover
parsley	partisan	passport
parsnip	partisanship	password
parsimony	partition	paste
parsimonious	partner	pasteboard
parson	partnership	pastel
parsonage	partridge	pastern
part	party	pastime
apart	paschal	pastor
apartment	pass	pastoral
compartment	impassable	pastorate
department	passable	pastry
partake	passage	pasture
parterre	passageway	pasturage
partial	passed	patch
partiality	past	patchwork
partially	passenger	patchy

patella	patrimonial	pay
patent	patriot	paid
patentable	patriotic	payable
patented	patriotism	payee
patentee	patrol	payees
paternal	patrolman	paymaster
paternalism	patron	payment
paternally	patronage	repaid
paternity	patroness	repay
path	patronize	unpaid
pathfinder	patronymic	peace
pathless	pattern	pacify
pathway	patterned	peaceable
pathology	paucity	peaceful
pathos	pauper	peacemaker
pathetic	pauperism	peacock
patient	pauperization	peanut
impatient	pauperize	pearl
patience	pause	peasant
patio	pave	peasantry
patriarch	pavement	pebble
patriarchal	pavilion	pebbly
patriarchate	pawn	pecan
patrician	pawnbroker	peccant
patrimony	pawnshop	peccadillo

peccancy	pedigree	penalize
peccary	pediment	penalty
peck	pedometer	penology
pectoral	peer	penchant
peculate	peerage	pencil
peculiar	peeress	pendant
peculiarity	peerless	pendulous
peculiarly	peevish	pendulum
pecuniary	peg	penetrate
pedagogue	Pegasus	penetrability
pedagogic	pelican	penetrable
pedagogical	pelisse	penetrant
pedagogy	pellagra	penetration
pedal	pellet	penetrative
pedant	pellucid	penguin
pedantic	peltry	peninsula
pedantical	pelvis	peninsular
pedantry	pelvic	penitence
peddle	pemmican	impenitent
peddler	pen	penitent
pedestal	penholder	penitential
pedestrian	penknife	penitentiary
pedestrianism	penance	penitently
pediatrics	penal	pennant
pedicular	penalization	penny

penniless	perceive	perfidy
pension	imperceptible	perfidious
pensionary	perceptible	perforate
pensioner	perception	perforates
pensive	perceptive	perforation
pent	perceptual	perforator
pentagon	percentage	perforce
pentameter	perchance	perform
Pentecost	percolate	performable
penthouse	percolation	performance
penult	percolator	performer
antepenult	percussion	perfume
penultimate	percussive	perfumer
penumbra	perdition	perfumery
penury	peregrination	perfunctory
penurious	peremptory	perfunctorily
peon	peremptorily	perfunctoriness
peony	peremptoriness	perhaps
people	perennial	peril
pepper	perfect	imperiled
peppermint	imperfect	perilous
pepsin	perfectible	perimeter
peradventure	perfection	period
perambulate	perfectly	periodic
percale	pluperfect	periodical

periodicity	permit	persecute
peripatetic	permissibility	persecution
periphery	permissible	persecutor
periphrastic	permission	persevere
periscope	permutation	perseverance
perish	pernicious	Persian
imperishable	peroration	persiflage
perishable	peroxide	persimmon
peristyle	perpendicular	persist
peritoneum	perpetrate	persistence
peritonitis	perpetrates	persistency
periwinkle	perpetration	persistent
perjure	perpetrator	person
perjured	perpetual	impersonal
perjurer	perpetually	impersonate
perjures	perpetuate	personable
perjury	perpetuated	personage
permanent	perpetuation	personal
permanence	perpetuator	personality
permanently	perpetuity	personalize
permanganate	perplex	personally
permeate	perplexed	personalty
permeability	perplexedly	personification
permeable	perplexity	personify
permeation	perquisite	personnel

perspective	perturb	pestilent
perspicacious	disturb	pestilential
perspicacity	perturbation	pet
perspicuity	perturbed	petal
perspicuous	peruse	petite
perspire	perusal	petition
perspiration	Peruvian	petitioner
perspires	pervade	petrel
persuade	pervasion	petrify
dissuade	pervasive	petrifaction
persuaded	perverse	petrifactive
persuader	perversely	petrol
persuades	perversion	petroleum
persuasion	perversity	petticoat
persuasive	perversive	petty
persuasiveness	pervert	pettily
suasion	perverted	pettiness
pert	pervious	pettish
pertain	impervious	petulant
pertained	pessimism	petulance
pertinacious	pessimist	petunia
pertinacity	pessimistic	pew
pertinence	pest	pewter
pertinency	pesthouse	phaeton
pertinent	pestilence	phalanx

phantom	phlegm	phrenology
phantasm	phlegmatic	phthisis
pharmacy	phlox	phylactery
pharmaceutic	phonic	physic
pharmaceutical	phonetic	physical
pheasant	phonetician	physician
phenol	phonetics	physicist
phenomenon	phonograph	physics
phenomena	phosphorus	physiognomy
phenomenal	phosphate	physiology
phial	phosphide	physique
philanderer	phosphoresce	piano
philanthropy	phosphorescence	pianist
philanthropic	phosphorescent	piazza
philanthropical	photo-electric	pica
philanthropist	photograph	picaresque
philatelic	photogravure	piccolo
philharmonic	photolithograph	pick
philology	photomicrograph	pickax
philosophy	photoplay	picker
philosopher	photostat	picket
philosophic	phrase	pickle
philosophical	phraseology	picnic
philosophize	phrenetic	picture
philter	frantic	pictograph

pictorial	pilot	piscatorial
pictorially	pimento	pistachio
picturesque	pimple	pistol
piety	pin	piston
pig	pinafore	pit
piggery	pincers	pitfall
piggish	pinch	pitted
pig-headed	pine	pitch
pigeon	pineapple	pitcher
pigment	ping-pong	pith
pigmentation	pink	pittance
pike	pinnace	pity
pikestaff	pinnacle	piteous
pilaster	pipe	pitiable
pilchard	pipage	pitied
pile	pipe clay	pitiful
piled	piped	pitiless
pilgrim	pipette	pitilessness
pilgrimage	piquant	pivot
pillage	piquancy	pivotal
pillar	pique	placard
pillion	pirate	placate
pillory	piracy	placability
pillow	piratic	placable
pillowcase	pirouette	place

placeman	plantation	plaudit
placement	planted	plausible
placer	planter	plausibility
placid	supplant	play
placidity	transplant	player
plagiarism	plantain	playful
plagiarist	plaster	playgoer
plagiarize	plastered	playground
plagiary	plasterer	playhouse
plague	plastic	playmate
plain	plasticity	plaything
plainer	plate	playtime
plainly	plateau	playwright
plainness	plated	please
plaint	plateful	displease
plaintiff	platen	pleasant
plaintive	plater	pleasantly
plan	platform	pleasantness
planned	platinum	pleasantry
planet	platinate	pleasurable
planetoid	platinic	pleasure
plangent	platitude	unpleasant
plank	platitudinize	plebeian
plant	platitudinous	plebiscite
implant	platoon	plectrum

pledge		plucky		pocket	
pledgee		plug		pocketbook	
pledger		plumb		pocketknife	
pledgor		plumbed		poem	
plenty		plumber		poet	
plenarily		plumbic		poetaster	
plenary		plumbago		poetic	
plenipotentiary		plume		poetry	
plenitude		plumage		poignant	
plenteous		plump		poignancy	
plentiful		plunder		poinciana	
pleonasm		plunderer		poinsettia	
plethora		plunge		point	
plethoric		plunger		pointer	
pleura		pluperfect		pointless	
pleurisy		plural		points	
pliant		plurality		poise	
pliability		pluralize		poison	
pliable		plus		poisoned	
pliancy		plutocrat		poisoner	
plight		plutocracy		poisonous	
plow		plutocratic		poke	
plowshare		pneumatic		poker	
pluck		pneumatics		pole	
pluckily		pneumonia		polar	

polarity	polluted	pontiff
polarization	pollution	pontifical
polarize	polonaise	pontificate
polarizer	polonium	pontoon
polecat	poltroon	pony
polemic	polyandry	poor
polemical	polygamy	poorest
police	polyglot	poorhouse
policeman	polygon	poorly
policy	polygonal	poorness
policyholder	polyp	poplar
polish	pomade	poplin
polisher	pomegranate	popular
polite	pommel	depopulate
politely	pomology	populace
politeness	pompadour	popularity
politic	pompous	popularize
political	pomposity	popularly
politician	poncho	populate
politicly	pond	populous
politics	ponder	unpopular
polity	ponderable	porcelain
polka	ponderous	porch
pollen	pongee	porcupine
pollute	poniard	porphyry

porpoise	depose	post
porridge	expose	postage
porringer	impose	postal
port	poses	postcard
portable	propose	postdate
portage	suppose	posthaste
portal	position	postman
portcullis	deposition	postmark
porter	exposition	postmaster
porterhouse	imposition	poster
portfolio	preposition	posterior
porthole	proposition	posterity
portico	supposition	postern
portière	positive	postgraduate
portend	possess	posthumous
portent	dispossess	postilion
portentous	possession	postlude
portion	possessive	postpone
apportioned	possessor	postponement
portray	possessorship	postscript
portrait	possible	postulate
portraiture	impossible	postulant
portrayal	possibility	postulation
Portuguese	possibly	posture
pose	possum	pot

potter	pout	preamble
pottery	poverty	prearrange
potable	powder	prebendary
potation	powdery	precarious
potassium	power	precaution
potash	empower	precautionary
potato	powerful	precede
potent	powerless	precedence
impotent	practical	precedent
omnipotent	practicability	precedes
plenipotentiary	practicable	unprecedented
potency	practicality	precept
potentate	practically	preceptor
potential	practicalness	preceptress
potentiality	practice	precinct
potentially	practitioner	precious
potion	pragmatism	precipitate
pottage	pragmatic	precipice
pouch	pragmatist	precipitancy
poultice	prairie	precipitant
poultry	praise	precipitately
pounce	praised	precipitateness
pound	pray	precipitation
poundage	prayer	precipitous
poundcake	prayerful	precise

precision	predigestion	prelate
preclude	predilection	preliminary
preclusion	predispose	prelude
precocious	predisposition	premature
precocity	predominate	premeditate
preconceive	predominance	premeditation
preconception	predominant	premier
precursor	preeminent	premise
precursory	preempt	premium
predacious	preemption	premonition
depredation	preface	premonitory
predacity	prefatory	preoccupation
predatory	prefect	preoccupied
predecease	prefer	prepare
predecessor	preferability	preparedness
predestine	preferable	unprepared
predestination	preference	prepay
predetermine	preferential	prepaid
predicament	preferentially	prepayment
predicate	preferment	preponderate
predict	prefix	preponderance
predictable	prehistoric	preponderant
prediction	prejudge	preposition
unpredictable	prejudice	prepositional
predigest	prejudicial	prepossess

prepossession

preposterous

prerequisite

prerogative

presage

presbyterian

prescient

  nescient

  omniscient

  prescience

prescribe

  prescription

  prescriptive

present

  presence

  presentability

  presentable

  presentation

  presently

presentiment

preserve

  preservation

  preservative

  preserver

preside

presidency

president

presidential

press

  pressman

  pressure

  presswork

prestige

prestidigitator

presume

  presumable

  presumedly

  presumer

  presumption

  presumptive

  presumptuous

pretend

  pretended

  pretender

  pretense

  pretension

  pretentious

preterit

preternatural

  supernatural

pretext

pretty

  prettily

  prettiness

pretzel

prevail

  prevalence

  prevalent

prevaricate

  prevarication

  prevaricator

prevent

  preventability

  preventable

  prevention

  preventive

previous

prevision

price

  priced

  priceless

  prices

prickle

  prickly

pride

priest	printery	probate
priestess	prior	probation
priesthood	priority	probity
priestly	prism	problem
primal	prismatic	problematic
primary	prison	proceed
primarily	imprisoned	procedure
primate	prisoner	procession
primacy	pristine	processional
primeval	private	process
primitive	privacy	processes
primogeniture	privateer	proclaim
primordial	privately	proclamation
prince	privateness	proclivity
princeliness	privation	procrastinate
princely	deprive	procrastination
princess	privet	procrastinator
principal, principle	privilege	proctor
principality	privy	procure
principally	privily	procurable
unprincipled	privity	procuration
print	probable	procurement
printable	improbable	prodigal
printed	probability	prodigality
printer	probably	prodigy

prodigious	profile	prohibitive
produce	profit	prohibitory
by-product	profitable	project
produced	profitless	projectile
producer	profligate	projection
produces	profligacy	projector
product	profound	proletarian
production	profoundness	proletariat
productive	profundity	prolific
productivity	profuse	prolix
profane	profusely	prolixity
profanation	profuseness	prologue
profanity	profusion	prolong
profess	progeny	prolongate
professed	progenitor	prolongation
profession	prognosis	promenade
professional	prognostic	prominent
professionalism	prognosticate	prominence
professionally	program	promiscuous
professor	progress	promiscuity
professorial	progression	promiscuously
professorship	progressive	promiscuousness
proffer	prohibit	promise
proficient	prohibition	promised
proficiency	prohibitionist	promissory

promontory	propellant	proponent
promote	propeller	proprietor
promoted	propulsion	proprietary
promoter	propensity	propriety
promotion	proper	prorate
prompt	property	pro rata
prompted	prophet	prorogue
prompter	prophecy	prosaic
promptitude	prophesy	proscenium
promptly	prophetic	proscribe
promptness	prophylactic	proscription
promulgate	propinquity	proscriptive
promulgation	propitiate	prosecute
pronoun	propitiation	prosecution
pronounce	propitiatory	prosecutor
pronounceable	propitious	proselyte
pronounced	proportion	prosody
pronouncement	disproportionate	prospect
pronunciation	proportionable	prospective
proof	proportional	prospector
propagate	proportionate	prospectus
propaganda	propose	prosper
propagandist	proposal	prospered
propagation	proposition	prosperity
propel	propound	prosperous

prostrate

prostration

protagonist

protect

protection

protectionist

protective

protector

protectorate

unprotected

protégé

protein

protest

Protestant

Protestantism

protestation

protocol

protoplasm

prototype

protoxide

protract

protraction

protractive

protractor

protrude

protrusion

protrusive

protuberance

protuberant

proud

prouder

proudest

proudly

prove

provable

proved

proven

proverb

proverbial

provide

improvident

providence

provident

providential

provider

provision

provisional

province

provincial

provincialism

provinciality

provincially

proviso

provisory

provoke

provocation

provocative

provost

proximate

approximate

proximity

proximo

proxy

prudent

imprudently

prudence

prudential

prurient

Prussian

psalm

psalmist

psalmody

pseudonym

psychic

psychiatrist

psychiatry	pulmonary	pungency
psychical	pulmotor	punish
psychoanalysis	pulpit	punishable
psychology	pulse	punished
psychopathic	pulsate	punishment
ptomaine	pulsation	punitive
public	pulsator	puny
publication	pulsatory	pupil
publicist	pulverize	purblind
publicity	pulverization	purchase
publicly	pulverizer	purchaser
publish	pumice	pure
publisher	pump	impure
pucker	pumpkin	purely
pudding	punch	purification
puddle	punctilio	purifier
pueblo	punctilious	purify
pugilism	punctual	purism
pugilist	punctuality	purist
pugilistic	punctually	Puritan
pugnacity	unpunctual	purity
pugnacious	punctuate	purge
puissant	punctuation	purgatory
puissance	puncture	purlieu
pullet	pungent	purloin

purloined	pursued	putrefactive
purple	pursuit	putrescence
purplish	purulent	putrescent
purport	purvey	putrid
purported	purveyance	putty
purpose	purveyor	puzzle
purposeful	purview	pygmy
purposeless	pusillanimity	pyorrhea
purposely	pusillanimous	pyramid
purse	pustule	pyramidal
purser	put	pyre
pursue	putative	pyrography
pursuance	putrefy	pyrometer
pursuant	putrefaction	pyrotechnics

Q

quackery

quadrangle

quadrant

quadruped

quadruple

quadruplex

quadruplicate

quagmire

quail

quaint

quaker

qualify

disqualify

qualification

qualified

qualitative

quality

unqualified

qualm

quantity

quantitative

quarantine

quarrel

quarrelsome

quarry

quart

quarter

quartered

quarterly

quartermaster

quartile

quartz

quatrain

quaver

quay

quayage

queen

queer

quench

quenchless

unquenchable

querulous

query

quest

question

questionable

questioned

questioner

questionnaire

unquestionable

unquestioned

quibble

quick

quicken

quicklime

quickness

quicksand

quicksilver

quick-witted

quiescent

quiet

quieted

quietly

quietness

quietude

quietus

quill

quilt

quinine

quinquennial

quintessence

quintet

quire

quirk

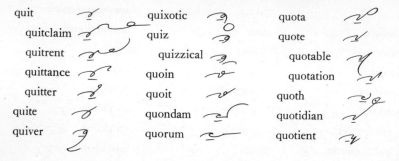

quit	quixotic	quota
quitclaim	quiz	quote
quitrent	quizzical	quotable
quittance	quoin	quotation
quitter	quoit	quoth
quite	quondam	quotidian
quiver	quorum	quotient

R

rabbi	radicalism	railway
rabbit	radically	raiment
rabble	radio	rain
rabid	radioactive	rainbow
rabies	radiogram	raindrop
raccoon	radiophone	rained
race	radiotelegraphy	rainfall
raced	radiotelephone	rainier
racer	radish	rainiest
racial	radium	raisin
racially	radius	ramble
racily	radial	rambler
raciness	radially	ramify
racket	radii	ramification
raconteur	radiuses	ramp
radiate	raffle	rampage
radiance	raft	rampant
radiancy	ragamuffin	rampart
radiant	raglan	ranch
radiated	ragout	rancher
radiation	raid	ranchero
radiator	rail	ranchman
radical	railhead	rancho
eradicate	raillery	rancid
	railroad	rancidly

rancor	rascality	rattle
rancorous	rascally	rattler
random	rash	rattlesnake
rank	rasher	rattly
rankle	rashest	raucous
ransack	rashly	ravage
ransom	rashness	ravel
rapacity	raspberry	raven
rapacious	rate	ravenous
rapid	rated	ravine
rapidity	rather	ravish
rapidly	ratify	raw
rapier	ratification	rawboned
rapport	ratio	rawhide
rapture	ratiocination	rawness
rapturous	ration	ray
rare	rational	rayless
rarefaction	irrational	react
rarefy	rationalism	reaction
rarely	rationalist	reactionary
rareness	rationalistic	reenact
rarer	rationalization	read
rarest	rationalize	readability
rarity	rationally	readable
rascal	rattan	reader

readjust	reason	recapitulate
readjustment	reasonable	recapture
readmission	reasoned	recast
ready	unreasonable	recede
readily	reassemble	recession
readiness	reassert	receipt
reaffirm	reassume	receive
reagent	reassure	receivability
real	rebate	receivable
realism	rebel	receiver
realist	rebellion	receivership
realistic	rebellious	receives
reality	rebind	recent
realizable	rebirth	reception
realization	reborn	receptacle
realize	rebound	receptive
really	rebuff	receptivity
realty	rebuild	recipient
unreal	rebus	recess
reanimate	rebut	recession
reappear	rebuttal	recessional
reappearance	rebutter	recessive
reappoint	recalcitrant	recharge
reargue	recall	recharged
rearrange	recant	recipe

reciprocate

reciprocal

reciprocation

reciprocative

reciprocator

reciprocity

recite

recital

recitation

recitative

recited

reck

reckless

reckon

reckoned

reckoner

reclaim

irreclaimable

reclaimable

reclaimed

reclamation

recline

reclination

reclined

recluse

recognize

recognition

recognizable

recognizance

unrecognized

recoil

recoiled

recollect

recollection

recommence

recommend

recommendation

recommendatory

recommit

recommitted

reconcile

irreconcilable

reconcilability

reconcilable

reconcilement

reconciliation

reconciliatory

recondite

reconnaissance

reconnoiter

reconquer

reconsider

reconstruct

reconstruction

reconstructive

record

recorded

recorder

recount

recounted

recoup

recoupment

recourse

recover

irrecoverable

recoverable

recovery

recreant

recreation

recriminate

recrimination

recriminative

recriminatory

recrudescence

recruit

recruited	redness	reelect
recrystallize	redeem	reelection
rectangle	irredeemable	reembark
rectangular	redeemer	reenact
rectify	redemption	reenacted
rectification	redemptory	reenforce
rectifier	unredeemed	reenforcement
rectilinear	redirect	reengage
rectitude	redistribute	reengrave
rector	redolent	reenlist
rectory	redolence	reenlistment
recumbent	redouble	reenter
recumbency	redoubt	reexamine
recuperate	redoubtable	reexamination
recuperation	redound	reexport
recuperative	reduce	refer
recuperatory	reduced	referable
recur	reducer	referee
recurrence	reduces	reference
recurrent	reducible	referendum
recusant	reduction	refine
red	redundant	refined
redden	redundance	refinement
reddened	redundancy	refiner
reddish	reecho	refinery

reflect	refrigerator	regatta
reflection	refuge	regenerate
reflective	refugee	regeneracy
reflector	refulgent	regeneration
reflex	refund	regenerative
reflexive	refunded	regenerator
reform	refurnish	unregenerate
reformation	refuse	regent
reformative	refusal	regicide
reformatory	refused	regimen
reformed	refuses	regiment
reformer	refute	regimental
refract	refutation	region
refraction	regain	regional
refractive	regained	register
refractivity	regal	registered
refractor	regally	registrar
refractory	regale	registration
refrain	regalia	registry
refrained	regard	regnant
refresh	disregard	regret
refreshment	regardful	regretful
refrigerate	regardless	regrettable
refrigeration	regards	regular
refrigerative	unregarded	irregular

regularity	rejoice	relentless
regulate	rejoiced	relevant
regulatory	rejoices	irrelevant
regurgitate	rejoin	relevance
regurgitation	rejoinder	relevancy
rehabilitate	rejuvenate	reliable
rehabilitation	rejuvenation	reliability
rehearse	rejuvenescence	reliance
rehearsal	rekindle	self-reliant
reimburse	relapse	unreliable
reimbursement	relate	relief
reimport	related	relievable
reimportation	relation	religion
reincarnation	relational	irreligious
reindeer	relationship	religious
reinstate	relative	relinquish
reinsure	relativity	relinquishment
reinvigorate	relax	relish
reissue	relaxation	reluctant
reiterate	relaxed	reluctance
reiteration	relaxes	remain
reject	release	remainder
dejected	relegate	remained
eject	relegation	remand
rejection	relent	remark

remarkable	remonstration	renunciatory
remarry	remonstrative	renovate
remedy	remorse	renovated
irremediable	remorseful	renovation
remediable	remorseless	renown
remedial	remote	renowned
remember	remoteness	rent
remembrance	remount	rental
remind	remove	rented
reminder	irremovable	reopen
remindful	removable	reorder
reminiscent	removal	reorganize
reminiscence	remunerate	repair
remiss	remuneration	irreparable
remission	remunerative	repaired
remit	renaissance	reparable
remittal	render	reparation
remittance	rendition	reparative
remittent	renegade	repartee
remitter	renew	repast
remnant	renewable	repatriate
remonstrate	renewal	repay
remonstrance	renominate	repaid
remonstrant	renounce	repayment
remonstrates	renunciation	repeal

repealed	replant	unrepresented
repeat	replanted	repress
repeatedly	replenish	irrepressible
repeater	replenishment	repression
repetition	replete	repressive
repel	repletion	reprieve
repelled	replevin	reprimand
repellence	replica	reprint
repellent	reply	reprisal
repulse	report	reproach
repent	reporter	irreproachable
repentance	repose	reproachful
repentant	reposeful	reprobate
repented	reposes	reprobation
repercussion	repository	reproduce
repercussive	repossess	reproduced
repertoire	reprehend	reproducer
repertory	reprehensibility	reproduces
repetition	reprehensible	reproduction
repetitious	reprehension	reproductive
repine	reprehensive	reprove
repined	represent	reproof
replace	misrepresent	reptile
replaced	representation	reptilian
replacement	representative	republic

republican	requital	residential
republicanism	reredos	residue
republish	resale	residual
repudiate	resold	residuary
repudiated	rescind	residuum
repudiation	rescript	resign
repugnant	rescue	resignation
repugnance	rescued	resigned
repulse	rescuer	resignedly
repulsed	research	resilient
repulsion	resemble	resilience
repulsive	resemblance	resiliency
repurchase	resent	resin
repute	resented	resist
disrepute	resentful	irresistible
reputable	resentment	resistance
reputation	reserve	resistant
request	reservation	resistibility
requiem	reserved	resistible
require	reservoir	resistivity
requirement	reship	resistless
requires	reside	resolve
requisite	residence	irresolute
requisition	residency	resoluble
requite	resident	resolute

resolution	respirator	restrained
resolvable	respiratory	restraint
resolved	respite	unrestrained
resolvent	resplendent	restrict
resonant	resplendence	restriction
resonance	resplendency	restrictive
resonator	respond	unrestricted
resort	respondent	result
resorted	response	resultant
resound	irresponsibility	results
resounded	irresponsible	resume
resource	responsible	resumable
resourceful	responsive	resumption
respect	rest	résumé
disrespect	rested	resurgent
irrespective	restful	resurgence
respectability	restless	resurrect
respectable	rests	resurrected
respecter	restate	resurrection
respectful-ly	restaurant	resuscitate
respective	restitution	resuscitation
respects	restore	retail
respire	restoration	retailed
respirable	restorative	retailer
respiration	restrain	retain

retained	retraceable	return
retainer	retract	returnable
retention	retractile	reunion
retentive	retraction	reunite
retentivity	retractive	revalue
retaliate	retractor	reveal
retaliation	retreat	revelation
retaliative	retreated	revelry
retaliatory	retrench	revenge
retard	retrenchment	revenged
retardation	retrial	revengeful
retell	retribution	revenue
reticent	retributive	reverberate
reticence	retrieve	reverberant
reticule	irretrievable	reverberation
retina	retrievable	reverberative
retinal	retriever	reverberator
retinue	retroactive	reverberatory
retire	retrocession	revere
retired	retrograde	irreverent
retirement	retrogression	reverence
retires	retrogressive	reverend
retort	retrospect	reverent
retouch	retrospection	reverential
retrace	retrospective	reverently

reverie	revivification	rhetorical
reverse	revivify	rhetorician
reversal	survive	rheumatism
reverses	revoke	rheumatic
reversible	irrevocable	rheumatoid
reversion	revocable	rhinestone
reversionary	revocation	rhinitis
revert	revolt	rhinoceros
revertible	revolve	rhubarb
revetment	revolution	rhythm
revictual	revolutionary	rhythmic
review	revolutionist	rhythmical
reviewed	revolutionize	ribald
reviewer	revolver	ribaldry
revile	revulsion	ribband
reviled	revulsive	ribbon
revilement	reward	rich
revise	rewarded	enrich
reviser	rewrite	richer
revision	rhapsody	riches
revisit	rhapsodic	richest
revitalize	rhapsodist	richly
vitalization	rhapsodize	richness
revive	rheostat	ride
revival	rhetoric	ridden

rider	ringer	ritually
riderless	ringleader	rival
ridicule	ringlet	rivalry
ridiculous	ringmaster	river
riffraff	riot	riverside
rifle	rioted	rivet
rifled	riotous	road
rifleman	riparian	roadbed
right	ripe	roadstead
right-angled	ripen	roadster
righteous	ripened	roadway
righteousness	ripeness	roam
rightful	riper	roamed
right-hand	ripest	roamer
rightly	ripple	roast
rightness	ripsaw	roaster
rigid	rise	robin
rigidity	arises	robust
rigidly	risen	rodent
rigor	risible	rodman
rigorous	risibility	rogue
ring	risk	roguery
ringbolt	rite	roguish
ringbone	ritual	roguishly
ringed	ritualistic	Roman

romance	rough	rubberize
romantic	roughcast	rubbery
romanticism	roughdry	rubbish
rondeau	roughen	rubicund
rookery	rougher	ruble
room	roughest	ruddy
roomer	roughhew	ruddily
roomful	roughly	ruddiness
roommate	roughness	rude
roomy	roulette	rudely
rosary	round	rudeness
rot	roundhouse	ruder
rotten	roundly	rudiment
rottenness	roundness	rudimental
rotate	roundsman	rudimentary
rotary	rout	rueful
rotation	route	ruffian
rotative	routed	ruffle
rotator	routine	ruffled
rotatory	royal	ruin
rotor	royalism	ruination
rotund	royally	ruined
rotunda	royalty	ruinous
rotundity	rub	rule
rouge	rubber	ruled

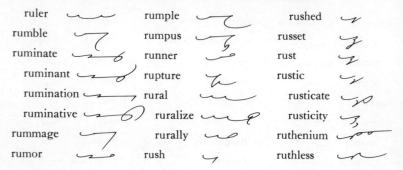

ruler	rumple	rushed
rumble	rumpus	russet
ruminate	runner	rust
ruminant	rupture	rustic
rumination	rural	rusticate
ruminative	ruralize	rusticity
rummage	rurally	ruthenium
rumor	rush	ruthless

S

Sabbath

sabbatical

sable

saccharin

sacerdotal

sachem

sachet

sacrament

sacramental

sacred

sacrifice

sacrificial

sacrilege

sacrilegious

sacristy

sacristan

sacrosanct

sad

sadden

sadness

safe

safe-conduct

safeguard

safe-keeping

safely

safeness

safety

unsafe

saffron

sagacity

sagacious

sahib

saint

sainted

saintliness

saintly

salad

salamander

salary

salaried

sale

resale

salability

salable

salesman

wholesale

salient

salience

saline

saliva

salivate

salivation

salmon

salon

saloon

salt

saltcellar

salted

saltpeter

salty

salubrious

salute

salutary

salutation

salutatorian

salutatory

salvage

salvation

salve

same

sameness

samovar

sample

example

exemplar	sapphire	satirize
sampler	saraband	satisfy
sanatory	sarcasm	dissatisfy
sanatorium	sarcastic	satisfaction
sanctify	sarcoma	satisfactory
sanctification	sarcophagus	unsatisfactory
sanctimonious	sarcophagi	saturate
sanction	sardine	saturation
sanctitude	sardonic	saturnine
sanctity	sardonyx	sauce
sanctuary	sarsaparilla	saucepan
sanctum	sartorial	saucer
sand	sassafras	saucily
sandal	satanic	sauciness
sane	satchel	saucy
insane	satiate	sauerkraut
sanity	insatiable	saunter
sanguine	satiable	sausage
consanguinity	satiation	savage
sanguinary	satiety	savagely
sanitary	satin	savagery
insanitary	satire	savanna
sanitation	satiric	save
sapient	satirical	savable
saponify	satirist	saved

savior	scapular	scherzo
savor	scarab	schism
saw	scarce	schismatic
sawdust	scarcity	schist
sawhorse	scarf	school
sawn	scarify	scholar
sawyer	scarification	scholarly
Saxon	scarlatina	scholarship
saxophone	scarlet	scholastic
scabbard	scatter	scholasticism
scaffold	scattered	schoolbook
scald	scavenger	schoolboy
scallop	scenario	schoolhouse
scalp	scene	schoolmaster
scalpel	scenery	schoolroom
scandal	scenic	schooner
scandalization	scenical	sciatica
scandalize	scent	science
scandalous	scented	scientific
Scandinavian	scepter	scientist
scansion	schedule	scimitar
scant	scheme	scintilla
scantily	schematic	scintillant
scantiness	schematize	scintillate
scapula	schemer	scintillation

scion	scrupulous	unseasonable
scissors	unscrupulous	secede
scoff	scrutiny	secession
scoffer	scrutinize	secessionist
scope	scuffle	seclude
scorch	scullion	secluded
score	sculptor	seclusion
scorn	sculptural	second
scorned	sculpture	secondarily
scornful	scum	secondary
scorpion	scurrility	seconded
Scotch	scurrilous	seconder
scoundrel	scurvy	secondly
scourge	scythe	secret
scraper	seal	secrecy
scrawl	sealed	secreted
screw	sealskin	secretion
scribble	search	secretive
script	research	secretly
scriptural	searcher	secretory
scripture	searchlight	secretary
scroll	season	secretarial
scrub	seasonable	secretariat
scruple	seasonal	sect
scrupulosity	seasoned	nonsectarian

sectarian	seducible	selection
sectary	seduction	selective
section	seductive	selectivity
sectional	sedulous	selectman
sectionalism	seemly	selector
sectionalize	unseemly	selenium
sectionally	seepage	self
sector	seersucker	self-assertion
secular	seethe	self-assured
secure	segment	self-command
securely	segmental	self-complacency
security	segmentary	self-conceit
sedan	segmentation	self-confidence
sedate	segregate	self-conscious
sedateness	segregation	self-contained
sedative	seismograph	self-contradiction
sedentary	seismology	self-contradictory
sediment	seize	self-control
sedimentary	seizable	self-deceit
sedimentation	seized	self-defense
sedition	seizes	self-denial
seditious	seizure	self-destruction
seduce	seldom	self-determined
seducer	select	self-educated
seduces	selected	self-esteem

self-evident	self-sufficient	senatorially
self-examination	self-supporting	senatorship
self-executing	self-surrender	send
self-government	selvage	godsend
self-importance	semantics	missent
self-induced	semaphore	sender
self-indulgence	semblance	sent
self-interest	semester	senile
selfish	semiannual	senility
selfishness	semicircle	senior
unselfish	semicircular	seniority
self-love	semicivilized	sensate
self-made	semicolon	insensate
self-perception	semidetached	sensation
self-possessed	semifinal	sensational
self-reliance	seminar	sensationalism
self-renunciation	seminary	sensationally
self-reproach	semiofficial	sense
self-respect	semiopaque	senseless
self-restraint	semiprecious	sensibility
self-righteous	semitransparent	sensible
self-sacrifice	semiweekly	sensitive
self-satisfied	senate	sensitivity
self-starter	senator	sensitization
self-styled	senatorial	sensitize

sensitizer		separation		serenata	
sensory		separatist		serene	
sensual		separative		serenely	
sensualism		separator		sereneness	
sensuality		sepia		serenity	
sensually		sepoy		serf	
sensuous		sepsis		serge	
sentence		septic		sergeant	
sententious		antiseptic		serial	
sentient		sepulcher		serially	
sentience		sepulchral		series	
sentiency		sepulture		serious	
sentiment		sequel		seriousness	
sentimental		sequence		sermon	
sentimentalism		sequester		sermonize	
sentimentalist		sequestered		serpent	
sentimentality		sequestrate		serpentine	
sentimentalize		sequestration		serum	
sentimentally		sequin		serous	
sentinel		Sequoia		serve	
sentry		seraph		servant	
separate		seraphic		served	
separability		seraphim		server	
separable		Serbian		service	
separately		serenade		serviceable	

servile		sextant		shamble	
servility		sextet		shame	
servitor		sexton		shamefaced	
servitude		shabby		shameful	
sesame		shabbily		shameless	
session		shabbiness		shampoo	
settee		shackle		shamrock	
settle		shade		shanghai	
settled		shadier		shank	
settlement		shadiest		shan't	
settler		shadily		shape	
unsettled		shadiness		shaped	
sever		shadow		shapeless	
severable		shadowy		shapeliness	
severance		shady		shapely	
several		shaft		shaper	
severalty		shake		share	
severe		shaker		shared	
severity		shakily		shareholder	
sew		shakiness		sharer	
sewed		Shakespearean		shark	
sewn		shall		sharp	
sewer		shallow		sharpen	
sewage		shallowly		sharpened	
sewerage		shallowness		sharpener	

sharper	sherbet	shiver
sharpest	sheriff	shock
sharpness	sherry	shoddy
sharpshooter	shiftless	shoe
sharp-witted	shilling	shoes
shatter	shimmer	shoot
non-shatterable	shimmery	shot
shattered	shingle	shop
shear	ship	shopkeeper
sheared	reship	shoplifter
shears	shipboard	shopper
sheath	shipbuilder	shopworn
sheepish	shipload	workshop
sheer	shipmate	short
sheerer	shipment	shortage
sheerest	shipowner	shortcake
sheerly	shipper	shortcoming
sheerness	shipshape	shorten
shelf	shipwreck	shorter
shelves	shipwright	shortest
shellac	shipyard	shorthand
shellfish	unship	short-lived
shelter	shire	shortly
sheltered	shirk	shortness
shelterless	shirt	shortsighted

shortstop	shunt	sidewalk
should	shut	sight
shoulder	shutdown	sightless
shovel	shutter	sightliness
shower	shy	sightly
showy	shied	sight-seeing
showily	shier	unsightly
showiness	shiest	signal
shrewd	shyly	signaler
shrift	shyness	signalize
shrine	sibilant	signally
shrink	sibyl	signature
shrank	sick	signatory
shrinkage	sickened	unsigned
shrive	sickliness	signify
shriven	sickly	insignificant
shroud	sickness	significant
shrub	side	significantly
shrug	beside	signification
shudder	sideboard	silence
shuddered	sidelong	silencer
shuffle	sidepiece	silent
shuffled	sides	silhouette
shun	sidestep	silicon
shunned	sidetrack	silica

silicate	since	sirloin
silk	sincere	sirup
silken	insincere	sister
silkiness	sincerely	sisterhood
silkworm	sincerity	sister-in-law
silt	sinecure	sisterly
silver	sinew	situation
silversmith	sinewy	situated
silverware	singer	size
silvery	single	sizable
simian	singleness	sizes
similar	singly	skeleton
similarity	singular	skeletonize
simile	singularity	skeptic
similitude	singularly	skeptical
simple	sinister	skepticism
simpler	sinner	sketch
simplest	sinuous	sketchily
simplicity	sinuosity	skewer
simplification	sinus	skill
simplify	siphon	skilled
simply	siphoned	skillful
simulate	sir	unskillful
dissimulation	sire	skirmish
simultaneous	siren	skirt

sky		sleep		slipshod	
skies		sleeper		sloop	
skylark		sleepily		sloth	
skylight		sleepiness		slothful	
skyrocket		sleepless		slouch	
skyscraper		slept		slough	
skyward		slender		slovenly	
slack		slenderer		slow	
slacken		slenderest		slower	
slackness		slenderness		slowest	
slander		slice		slowly	
slanderer		slight		slowness	
slanderous		slighter		sludge	
slant		slightest		sluggard	
slanted		slightly		sluggish	
slatternly		slightness		sluice	
slaughter		sliminess		sluiceway	
slaughtered		slimily		slumber	
slaughterer		slimness		slumberer	
slaughterhouse		sling		slumberous	
slave		slip		slung	
enslavement		slipknot		underslung	
slaveholder		slippage		slur	
slavery		slipper		slush	
slavish		slipperiness		sly	

slier	smoothed	snuffle
sliest	smoothen	soak
slyly	smoother	soap
small	smoothest	soapiness
smaller	smoothness	sober
smallest	smother	social
smallness	smothered	sociability
smallpox	smudge	sociable
smart	smuggle	socialism
smarten	smuggled	socialist
smarter	snapshot	socialistic
smartest	snarl	socialization
smartly	sneer	socialize
smartness	snort	socially
smelt	snout	society
smile	snow	sociology
smiles	snowball	sodden
smite	snowfall	sodium
smoke	snowflake	soda
smokeless	snowplow	sofa
smoker	snowshoe	soft
smokestack	snowslide	soften
smokiest	snowstorm	softness
smolder	snowy	soil
smooth	snuff	sojourn

sojourned	solidity	somewhere
sojourner	solidly	somnambulism
solace	solidness	somnambulist
solar	soliloquy	somnolent
solder	soliloquize	sonata
soldier	solitaire	song
soldierly	solitary	songster
soldiery	solitude	son-in-law
solecism	solstice	sonnet
solemn	solution	sonorous
solemnity	solubility	sonority
solemnization	soluble	soon
solemnize	solve	sooner
solemnly	solvable	soonest
solenoid	solvent	soothe
solicit	solvency	soothed
solicitation	somber	sophisticate
solicitor	some	sophistication
solicitous	somebody	sophistry
solicitude	somehow	sophomore
unsolicited	someone	soporific
solid	something	soprano
solidarity	sometime	sorcery
solidification	sometimes	sorcerer
solidify	somewhat	sordid

sordidness	southeast	spasmodically
sorority	southeasterly	speak - speech
sorrow	southeastern	bespeak
sorrowful	southerly	speaker
sorry	southerner	spoke
sort	southernmost	spoken
assorted	southwest	unspeakable
sorted	southwesterly	special
sought	souvenir	especial
unsought	sovereign	specialist
soul	sovereignty	specialization
soulful	space	specialize
soulless	spacious	specially
sound	spandrel	specialty
sounded	spangle	specific
soundest	spaniel	specification
soundless	Spanish	specify
soundly	spare	unspecified
soundness	spared	specie
unsound	spark	species
soup	sparkle	specimen
source	sparse	specious
resourceful	sparsity	spectacle
sources	spasm	spectacular
south	spasmodic	spectacularly

spectator	sphinx	spiritualize
specter	spice	spiritually
spectral	spiciness	spirituous
spectroscope	spider	spite
spectrum	spidery	despite
speculate	spigot	spiteful
speculum	spike	splendor
speech	spill	splendid
speechless	spilled	splendorous
speechmaker	spillway	splint
speed	spin	splinter
speedily	spinster	spoil
speedometer	spun	spoilage
speedway	spinach	spoiled
spell	spine	spoliate
misspell	spinal	spoliation
speller	spineless	spoliative
spend	spinet	spoliator
misspent	spiral	sponge
spendthrift	spire	sponsor
spermaceti	spirit	spontaneity
sphere	spiritless	spontaneous
hemisphere	spiritualism	spoon
spherical	spiritualist	spoonful
spheroid	spirituality	tablespoon

teaspoon	squad	stability
sport	squadron	stabilization
sportive	squall	stabilize
sportsman	squalor	stabilizer
sportsmanship	squalid	stable
spot	squalidity	staccato
spotless	squander	stadium
spotlight	square	stadia
spotted	squash	stadiums
spouse	squat	staff
sprawl	squatter	staves
sprightly	squaw	stage
spring	squeak	stagecoach
sprinkle	squeal	stagecraft
sprinkled	squeamish	stagger
sprinkler	squeegee	stagnate
sprocket	squeeze	stagnant
sprout	squeezed	stagnation
spunk	squib	stain
spur	squid	stained
spurious	squint	stair
spurn	squirm	staircase
spurt	squirrel	stairway
spy	squirt	stalactite
spied	stabile	stalagmite

stalk	stapler	stately
stallion	star	statement
stalwart	starfish	stateroom
stamina	starlight	statesman
stammer	starry	static
stammerer	starch	hydrostatics
stamp	stare	station
stampede	stared	stationary
stanch	stark	stationer
stanchion	starling	stationery
stand	start	statistics
notwithstanding	started	statistical
stand-off	startle	statistically
standpipe	startled	statistician
standpoint	starve	statue
standstill	starvation	statuary
stood	starved	statuesque
understood	state	statuette
withstand	estate	stature
withstood	instate	status
standard	misstatement	statute
standardization	reinstate	statutory
standardize	statehood	stay
stanza	statehouse	stayed
staple	stateliness	stead

instead	stein	sternly
steadfast	stellar	sternness
steady	stem	sternum
steadily	stemmed	stertorous
steadiness	stencil	stethoscope
unsteady	stenography	stevedore
steal	stenographer	stew
stolen	step	steward
stealth	stepchild	stick
stealthier	stepdaughter	sticker
stealthily	stepladder	stickful
steam	stepmother	stickier
steamboat	stepson	stickiest
steamed	stereopticon	stickiness
steamer	stereoscope	sticky
steamship	stereotype	stiff
steamy	sterilize	stiffen
steel	sterile	stiffer
steep	sterility	stiffest
steeper	sterilization	stiffness
steepest	sterilizer	stifle
steeple	sterling	stigma
steer	stern	stigmas
steerage	sterner	stigmata
steersman	sternest	stigmatic

stigmatism	stirrup	stone
stigmatize	stitch	stoned
stile	stock	stoneware
stiletto	stockade	stonework
still	stockbroker	stonily
distill	stockholder	stoniness
stillness	stockily	stony
stilly	stockiness	stood
stilt	stockings	stool
stilted	stockman	stoop
stimulate	stock-still	stop
stimulant	stocky	stoppage
stimulus	stockyard	stopped
sting	stogy	stopper
stinger	stoic	store
stung	stoical	storage
stint	stoicism	storehouse
stinted	stoke	storeroom
stipend	stokehold	stork
stipendiary	stoker	storm
stipple	stole	stormed
stippled	stolid	stormier
stipulate	stolidity	stormiest
stir	stolidly	stormily
stirred	stomach	storminess

stormy	strait-laced	strawberry
stout	strange	strawboard
stouter	estranged	streak
stoutest	strangely	streakily
stoutly	strangeness	streakiness
stoutness	stranger	streaky
stow	strangest	stream
stowage	strangle	streamed
stowaway	strangled	streamer
stowed	strangler	streamlet
straddle	strangles	streamline
straggle	strangulate	street
straggled	stratagem	strength
straggler	strategic	strengthen
straight	strategical	strengthened
straightedge	strategist	strenuous
straighten	strategy	stretch
straightened	stratify	stretcher
straightener	strata	strew
straightforward	stratification	strewn
straightway	stratum	striate
strait	stratums	striated
straiten	stratus	striation
straitened	substratum	strict
strait-jacket	straw	stricter

strictest	stroller	student
strictly	strong	studied
strictness	strength	studio
stricture	stronger	studious
stride	strongest	stuff
strident	stronghold	stuffier
strife	strongly	stuffiest
strike	strong-minded	stuffiness
striker	strontium	stuffy
stroke	structure	stultify
struck	structural	stultification
string	structurally	stumble
stringed	struggle	stump
stringier	struggler	stun
stringiest	strum	stunned
stringy	strummed	stunner
strung	strut	stunt
stringent	strutted	stunted
stringency	stub	stupefy
stripe	stubble	stupefacient
strive	stubborn	stupefaction
striven	stubbornness	stupor
strove	stucco	stupendous
stroll	stud	stupid
strolled	study	stupidity

stupidly	sub-basement	sublet
sturdy	subcellar	sublimate
sturdily	subcommittee	sublimated
sturdiness	subconscious	sublimation
sturgeon	subcontractor	sublime
stutter	subcutaneous	sublimer
style	subdeacon	sublimest
styled	subdivide	sublimity
stylish	subdivision	submarine
stylishness	subdue	submerge
stylist	subdued	submerged
stylistic	subeditor	submergence
stylographic	subequatorial	submerse
stylus	subgroup	submersible
styptic	subhead	submersion
Styx	subject	submit
suasion	subjection	submission
suave	subjective	submissive
suavely	subjectivity	submitted
suavity	subjoin	subnormal
subacid	subjugate	subofficer
subagent	subjugation	suborder
subaltern	subjugator	subordinate
subaqueous	subjunctive	coordinate
subarctic	sublease	subordination

subordinative	substantiation	subvert
suborn	substantive	subversion
subornation	substitute	subversive
suborner	substitution	subway
subpœna	substratum	succeed
subscribe	substrata	succeeded
subscriber	subtend	success
subscription	subterfuge	successful
subsequent	subterranean	succession
subserve	subtitle	successive
subservience	subtle	successor
subservient	subtile	unsuccessful
subside	subtler	succinct
subsidence	subtlest	succor
subsidy	subtlety	succotash
subsidiary	subtly	succulent
subsidize	subtract	succulence
subsist	subtraction	succumb
subsistence	subtrahend	such
subsists	subtreasury	suction
subsoil	subtropical	sudden
substance	suburb	suddenly
substantial	suburban	suddenness
substantially	suburbanite	sudorific
substantiate	subvention	sue

suable	sugary	sultry
sued	suggest	sum
sues	suggestibility	summation
suede	suggestible	summed
suet	suggestion	sumac
suffer	suggestive	summary
sufferable	suicide	summarily
sufferance	suicidal	summariness
sufferer	suit	summarization
suffice	suitability	summarize
insufficient	suitable	summer
sufficiency	suited	summerhouse
sufficient	suite	summery
suffix	sulk	summit
suffocate	sulkily	summon
suffocation	sulkiness	sumptuous
suffocative	sullen	sumptuary
suffragan	sullenness	sun
suffrage	sulphur	sunbeam
suffragette	sulphate	sunburn
suffragist	sulphide	sunburst
suffuse	sulphite	sundial
suffusion	sulphuric	sunless
sugar	sulphurous	sunlight
sugarplum	sultan	sunned

sunniness	superficially	supervene
sunrise	superfluous	supervention
sunset	superfluity	supervise
sunshine	superhuman	supervision
sunstroke	superimpose	supervisor
Sunday	superinduce	supervisory
sunder	superintend	supine
asunder	superintendence	supineness
sundry	superintendent	supper
sunk	superior	supplant
sunken	superiority	supplanted
superable	superlative	supple
insuperable	supernal	supplement
superabundant	supernatural	supplemental
superannuate	preternatural	supplementary
superannuation	supernaturalism	supplicate
superb	supernaturally	suppliant
supercalender	supernumerary	supplicant
supercargo	supersaturate	supplication
supercilious	superscribe	supplicatory
superdreadnaught	superscription	supply
supereminent	supersede	supplied
supererogation	supersensitive	support
superficial	superstition	supportable
superficiality	superstitious	supported

supporter	surf	surround
suppose	surface	surroundings
supposable	surfeit	survey
supposedly	surge	surveillance
supposition	surgeon	surveyor
supposititious	surgery	survive
suppress	surgical	revive
suppression	surly	survival
suppressive	surlier	survivorship
suppurate	surliest	susceptible
suppuration	surmise	susceptibility
suppurative	surmised	suspect
supreme	surmount	suspicion
supremacy	surmountable	suspicious
surbase	surmounted	unsuspected
surcease	surname	suspend
surcharge	surpass	suspended
surcingle	surplice	suspender
sure	surplus	suspense
surely	surplusage	suspension
sureness	surprise	sustain
surer	surprised	sustainable
surest	surrender	sustained
surety	surreptitious	sustenance
suretyship	surrogate	suture

suzerain	sweeten	swirl
suzerainty	sweetheart	Swiss
swagger	sweetish	switch
swain	sweetmeat	swivel
swallow	sweetness	swollen
swamp	swell	swoon
swan	swelled	swoop
swarm	swelter	sword
swarthy	swerve	swordfish
swarthier	swift	swordsman
swarthiest	swifter	sycamore
swastika	swiftest	sycophant
swath	swiftly	sycophancy
swathe	swiftness	sycophantic
sway	swill	syllable
swear	swim	syllabi
sweat	swam	syllabic
sweatily	swum	syllabicate
sweatiness	swindle	syllabication
sweatshop	swindler	syllabification
Swedish	swine	syllabify
sweep	swineherd	syllabus
sweet	swing	syllabuses
sweetbread	swung	syllogism
sweetbrier	swipe	syllogistic

symbol	symptom	synonym
symbolic	symptomatic	synonymous
symbolical	symptomatology	synopsis
symbolism	synagogue	synoptic
symbolist	synchronize	syntax
symbolization	synchronism	synthesis
symbolize	synchronous	synthesist
symmetry	syncopate	synthesize
symmetric	syncopation	synthetic
symmetrical	syncope	synthetical
sympathize	syndic	syringe
sympathetic	syndicalism	syrup
sympathizer	syndicate	system
sympathy	synecdoche	systematic
symphony	synod	systematical
symphonic	synodic	systematize
symposium	synodical	systemic

T

tabard

tabasco

tabernacle

table

  tableau

  tablecloth

  tablespoon

  tablet

  tableware

  tabloid

taboo

taboret

tabulate

  tabular

  tabularize

tachometer

tacit

  taciturn

  taciturnity

tackle

tact

  tactful

  tactile

  tactility

tactless

tactics

  tactical

  tactician

taffeta

tailor

taint

  tainted

take

  overtake

  takedown

  taken

  take-off

  took

  undertake

talent

  talented

talisman

talk

  talkative

  talker

tall

  taller

  tallest

  tallness

tamarack

tamarind

tambourine

tame

  tamely

  tamer

  tamest

  untamed

tamper

tanager

tandem

tang

tangent

  tangential

  tangerine

tangible

  intangible

  tangibility

tangle

  disentangle

  entangle

tank

  tankage

  tankard

  tanker

tanner	tart	tautology
tannery	tartan	tavern
tannic	tartar	tawdry
tantalize	tartaric	tawny
tantalization	task	tax
tantalum	tassel	taxable
tantamount	tasseled	taxation
taper	taste	taxed
tapestry	tasted	taxes
tapioca	tasteful	taxi
tapir	tasteless	taxicab
tappet	taster	taximeter
tarantula	tastily	taxidermy
tarantella	tastiness	taxidermist
tardy	tasty	teach
tardier	tatter	taught
tardiest	tattered	teachability
tardily	tatters	teachable
target	tattle	teacher
tariff	tattoo	team
tarlatan	tattooed	teamster
tarnish	taunt	teamwork
untarnished	taunted	tear
tarpaulin	taut	tearful
tarpon	tautness	tearless

tears		telephone		tempestuous	
tear		telephonic		template	
tore		telephonically		temple	
torn		telephony		templed	
tease		telescope		tempo	
teased		telescopic		temporal	
teaspoon		telescopical		temporality	
teaspoonful		tell		temporary	
technic		telltale		temporarily	
technical		told		temporization	
technicality		tellurium		temporize	
technician		temblor		temporizer	
technique		temerity		tempt	
technology		temerarious		temptation	
tedium		temper		tempted	
tedious		temperament		tempter	
telautograph		temperamental		temptress	
telegraph		temperamentally		tenable	
telegram		temperance		untenable	
telegrapher		intemperance		tenacity	
telegraphic		temperate		pertinacious	
telegraphical		temperately		pertinacity	
telegraphy		temperateness		tenacious	
telepathy		temperature		tenant	
telepathic		tempest		tenancy	

tenantable	tenser	terra cotta
tenanted	tensest	terrain
tenantless	tensile	terrapin
tenantry	tension	terrestrial
untenanted	tensional	terrify
tend	tensity	terrible
tended	tent	terrific
tendency	tentacle	terrifically
tender	tentative	territory
tendered	tenuity	territorial
tenderer	attenuated	territoriality
tenderest	tenuous	territorialize
tenderfoot	tepee	territorially
tenderloin	tepid	terror
tenderly	tercentenary	terrorism
tenderness	term	terrorist
tendon	termed	terroristic
tendril	terminable	terrorization
tenebrous	terminal	terrorize
tenement	terminally	terrorizer
tenet	terminate	terse
tennis	termination	terseness
tenon	terminology	terser
tenor	terminus	tersest
tense	terrace	tertiary

tessellate	texture	thenceforth
tessellation	than	thenceforward
test	thane	theocracy
tested	thank	theodolite
tester	thanked	theology
tests	thankful	theologian
untested	thankless	theory
testament	thanks	theorem
testamentary	thanksgiving	theoretic
testate	that	theorist
testator	thatch	theorize
testify	thaw	theorizer
testimonial	theater	theosophy
testimony	theatric	theosophic
tetanus	theatrical	theosophical
tether	theatricals	theosophist
tetragon	thee	therapy
tetragonal	theirs	therapeutic
tetralogy	theism	therapeutical
Teutonic	atheism	there
text	pantheism	thereabout
textbook	them	thereafter
textual	themselves	thereat
textually	then	thereby
textile	thence	therefore

therefrom		thickener		thinks	
therein		thicker		unthinkable	
thereinto		thicket		thirst	
thereof		thickly		thirstily	
thereon		thickness		thirstiness	
thereto		thief		thirsty	
theretofore		theft		this	
thereupon		thievery		thistle	
therewith		thievish		thither	
therm		thigh		thole	
thermal		thimble		thong	
thermion		thin		thoracic	
thermite		thinner		thorium	
thermometer		thinness		thorn	
thermometric		thinnest		thorough	
thermometrical		thing		thoroughbred	
thermostat		anything		thoroughfare	
thesaurus		everything		thoroughly	
these		nothing		thoroughness	
thesis		plaything		those	
theses		something		thou	
thew		things		though	
they		think		thought	
thick		thinkable		thoughtful	
thicken		thinker		thoughtless	

thousand	thrived	thus
thousandfold	throve	thwart
thousands	throat	thy
thousandth	throatiness	thine
thrall	throb	thyself
thrash	throne	thyme
thread	dethrone	thyroid
threadbare	enthroned	tiara
threadworm	throng	Tibetan
threat	throttle	tide
threaten	through	tidewater
threatened	throughout	tidy
three	throw	tidier
threnody	threw	tidiest
threshold	thrown	tidiness
threw	thrush	untidy
thrice	thrust	tiger
thrift	thud	tight
spendthrift	thug	air-tight
thriftily	thumb	tighten
thriftiness	thump	tightened
thriftless	thunder	tighter
thrifty	thunderbolt	tightest
thrill	thunderous	tiled
thrive	thundershower	till

until	tinsel	toasted
tilt	tint	toastmaster
tilted	tinted	tobacco
timber	tiny	toboggan
time	tinier	toccata
time-honored	tiniest	tocsin
timekeeper	tirade	today
timeless	tire	toga
timely	tired	together
timepiece	tireless	toil
timer	tiresome	toilful
time-table	tissue	toilsome
timid	titanium	token
intimidate	tithe	told
timidity	titillate	untold
timidly	titivate	tolerate
timorous	title	tolerable
tin	title-page	tolerance
tinware	titular	tolerant
tincture	titmouse	toleration
tinder	titrate	tomahawk
tinge	titration	tomato
tingle	toad	tomb
tinker	toadstool	tombstone
tinkle	toast	tomorrow

ton	topography	totalizer
tonnage	torch	totally
tone	torment	totem
monotone	tormented	totter
tonal	tormentor	touch
tonality	tornado	touchable
tongue	torpedo	touchdown
tonight	torpor	touchily
tonsil	torpid	touchiness
tonsillitis	torque	touchstone
tonsure	torrent	untouched
tonsorial	torrential	tough
tontine	torrentially	toughen
tool	torrid	toughened
tooth	torridity	tougher
teeth	torsion	tour
toothache	torso	tourist
toothed	tort	tourmaline
toothless	tortoise	tournament
toothpick	tortuous	tourniquet
toothsome	tortuosity	tousle
top	torture	toward
topaz	total	towel
topic	totality	tower
topical	totalization	town

township	toxic	toxicity	toxicology	trace	retrace	traceable	traced	tracer	tracery	trachea	trachoma	track	trackage	trackless	trackman	tract	tractable	traction	tractive	tractor	trade	traded	trade-mark	trader

township		tradesman		tranquilization
toxic		tradition		tranquilize
toxicity		traditional		tranquillity
toxicology		traditionally		tranquilly
trace		traduce		transact
retrace		traffic		transaction
traceable		tragedy		transatlantic
traced		tragedian		transcend
tracer		tragic		transcendence
tracery		tragical		transcendent
trachea		train		transcendental
trachoma		trained		transcribe
track		trainer		transcript
trackage		trainman		transcription
trackless		traitor		transcpt
trackman		traitorous		transfer
tract		traitress		transferable
tractable		trajectory		transference
traction		trammel		untransferable
tractive		trammeled		transfigure
tractor		tramp		transfiguration
trade		trample		transfix
traded		tramway		transform
trade-mark		trance		transformation
trader		tranquil		transformer

transfuse	transmission	transubstantiation
transfusion	transmittal	transverse
transgress	transmitter	transversal
transgression	transmogrify	trapeze
transgressor	transmute	trauma
transient	transmutability	traumatic
transience	transmutable	travail
transit	transmutation	travel
transition	transom	traveler
transitional	transparency	traverse
transitionally	transparent	travesty
transitive	transpire	treachery
transitory	transpiration	treacherous
translate	transplant	treacle
translatable	transplantation	tread
translation	transplanted	trod
translator	transport	trodden
untranslatable	transportable	treadle
transliterate	transportation	treason
obliterate	transported	treasonable
translucence	transpose	treasure
translucent	transposes	treasured
transmit	transposition	treasurer
transmissibility	transship	treasures
transmissible	transubstantiate	treasury

treat	triangulate	trillium
treatise	tribe	trilogy
treatment	tribal	trim
treaty	tribesman	trimly
treble	tribulation	trimmed
tremble	tribune	trimmer
tremendous	tribunal	trimness
tremolo	tribute	trinity
tremor	tributary	trinket
tremulous	trick	trio
trench	trickery	triphthong
trenchancy	trickily	triple
trenchant	trickiness	triplet
trencher	trickster	triplex
trepan	trickle	triplicate
trephine	trickled	triplication
trepidation	tricycle	triply
intrepid	trident	triptych
trespass	triennial	trisect
trespasser	trifle	trite
trestle	trifler	triturate
triad	trigger	trituration
trial	trigonometry	triumph
triangle	trigonometric	triumphal
triangular	trillion	triumphant

triumvirate	truckman	trustful
triune	truckle	untrustworthy
trivial	truculent	truth
triviality	truculence	truthful
trivially	trudge	untruthful
troche	true	try
trolley	trueness	trial
trombone	truer	untried
troop	truest	tryst
trooper	truism	tsar
tropic	truly	tub
tropical	truth	tuba
troth	untrue	tube
troubadour	trumpet	tubular
trouble	trumpeter	tuber
troublesome	truncate	tubercle
troublous	truncheon	tubercular
trousers	trundle	tuberculin
trousseau	trunk	tuberculosis
trout	trust	tuberculous
trowel	distrust	tuberose
truant	entrust	tuition
truancy	mistrust	intuition
truck	trustee	tumble
truckage	trusteeship	tumor

tumult	turncoat	two-ply
tumultuous	turned	twosome
tune	turnout	two-step
tuned	turnpike	type
tuneful	turnip	typesetter
tuneless	turpentine	typewriter
tuner	turpitude	typewritten
tungsten	turquoise	typist
tunic	turret	typographer
tunnel	turtle	typography
turban	tutelage	typothetae
turbid	tutor	typhus
turbidity	twaddle	typhoid
turbidly	tweezers	typify
turbulent	twilight	typical
turbulence	twin	typification
tureen	twine	tyrant
turgid	twinkle	tyrannical
turgidity	twirl	tyrannicide
turkey	twist	tyrannize
turmeric	two	tyrannous
turmoil	two-faced	tyranny
turn	twofold	tyro
turnbuckle	two-handed	tzar

U

ubiquity	unable	unassailable
ubiquitous	inability	unassisted
ugly	unabridged	unassuming
ugliness	unaccented	unattached
ukase	unacceptable	unattainable
ukulele	unaccompanied	unattained
ulcer	unaccountable	unattempted
ulcerate	unaccustomed	unattended
ulceration	unadjusted	unauthenticated
ulcerative	unadorned	unauthorized
ulcerous	unadulterated	unavailable
ulna	unaffected	unavoidable
ulnar	unaided	unaware
ulster	unalloyed	unbalanced
ulterior	unalterable	unbecoming
ultimate	un-American	unbelief
ultimatum	unamiable	unbelievable
ultimo	unanimity	unbend
ultramarine	unanimous	unbidden
ultra-violet	unanswerable	unblemished
umbrage	unappeasable	unblushing
umbrella	unapproachable	unbound
umlaut	unappropriated	unbreakable
umpire	unarmed	unbusinesslike
	unasked	uncanny

unceremonious	unconstitutional	undercurrent
uncertain	uncontradicted	underestimate
uncertainty	uncontrollable	underexpose
unchallenged	uncontrolled	undergarment
unchangeable	unconventional	undergo
uncharitable	uncouth	undergraduate
uncial	uncover	underground
uncivilized	unction	undergrowth
unclaimed	unctuous	underhanded
unclassified	uncultivated	underline
uncle	undamaged	undermine
unclean	undaunted	undermined
uncleaned	undeceive	underneath
uncollectible	undecided	underproduction
uncomfortable	undecipherable	underrate
uncommon	undefended	underscore
uncommunicative	undefiled	undersell
uncomplimentary	undeliverable	undersized
uncompromising	undemocratic	underslung
unconcerned	undemonstrative	understand
unconditional	undeniable	misunderstand
unconquerable	under	misunderstood
unconscionable	underbid	understudy
unconscious	underbrush	undertake
unconsidered	undercharge	undertaker

undertook
undervalue
underwrite
underwriter
undeserved
undesigned
undetermined
undeveloped
undigested
undignified
undimmed
undisciplined
undisclosed
undisguised
undismayed
undisposed
undisputed
undistinguishable
undisturbed
undivided
undo
undone
undoubted
undress
undulate

undulant
unduly
undutiful
undying
unearned
unearth
unearthly
uneasy
uneasily
uneasiness
uneatable
uneaten
uneducated
unembarrassed
unemployment
unencumbered
unending
unendorsed
unendurable
unenforceable
unenterprising
unenvied
unequaled
unequivocal
unerring

unethical
uneven
uneventful
unexaggerated
unexampled
unexcelled
unexceptionable
unexpected
unexpired
unexplored
unexpressed
unextinguished
unfaithful
unfamiliar
unfashionable
unfasten
unfavorable
unfeigned
unfinished
unfold
unforgettable
unforgivable
unfortified
unfortunate
unfrequented

unfriendly	unidiomatic	uninvited
unfruitful	uniform	union
unfulfilled	uniformity	unionism
unfurnished	unify	unionist
ungainly	unification	unionize
ungodly	unimaginable	unique
ungovernable	unimaginative	unison
ungracious	unimpaired	unissued
ungrateful	unimpeachable	unit
unguent	unimportant	Unitarian
unhampered	unimpressionable	unitary
unhandy	unindorsed	unite
unhappy	uninfluenced	united
unhardened	uninformed	unity
unharness	uninhabitable	universe
unhealthy	uninhabited	universality
unheard	uninitiated	universally
unhesitating	uninjured	university
unhinge	uninstructed	unjustifiable
unholy	unintelligent	unkind
unhonored	unintelligible	unkindliness
unhook	unintentional	unknightly
unhoped	unintentionally	unknit
unicorn	uninterested	unknown
unidentified	uninterrupted	unknowable

unknowing	unmitigated	unprecedented
unladylike	unmolested	unprejudiced
unlaundered	unmounted	unpremeditated
unlawful	unnamed	unprincipled
unlearn	unnatural	unprofessional
unleavened	unnecessary	unprofitable
unless	unnerve	unprogressive
unlettered	unnumbered	unpromising
unlicensed	unobjectionable	unpublished
unlike	unobservant	unpunctual
unlikely	unobtainable	unqualified
unlisted	unoccupied	unquestionable
unlovable	unopened	unquestioned
unlucky	unorganized	unquiet
unmailable	unorthodox	unreasonable
unmake	unostentatious	unrecognized
unman	unpaid	unredeemed
unmanageable	unpalatable	unrelated
unmannerly	unparalleled	unrepentant
unmarried	unpardonable	unreproved
unmask	unparliamentary	unrequired
unmerited	unpartisan	unresisting
unmindful	unpleasant	unrestrained
unmistakable	unpolished	unrestricted
unmistaken	unpopular	unrivaled

unruled	unsought	untidy
unruly	unsound	untidily
unsafe	unspeakable	until
unsaid	unspecified	unto
unsalable	unspoiled	untold
unsanctified	unspoken	untouched
unsatisfactory	unstained	untoward
unschooled	unstamped	untracked
unscrupulous	unsteadily	untroubled
unseasonable	unstinted	untrue
unseemly	unstrung	untruthful
unseen	unstudied	unusable
unselfish	unsubstantial	unused
unserviceable	unsuccessful	unusual
unsettled	unsuitable	unutterable
unship	unsung	unvarnished
unsightly	unsuspected	unversed
unsigned	unswerving	unwarrantable
unskilled	unsymmetrical	unwarranted
unskillful	unsystematic	unwary
unsociable	untainted	unwashed
unsoiled	untamed	unwavering
unsoldierly	untangle	unwelcome
unsolicited	untarnished	unwell
unsophisticated	unthinkable	unwholesome

unwieldy		uppermost		disuse	
unwilling		upright		misuse	
unwind		uproar		unused	
unwound		upset		usable	
unwise		upstairs		usage	
unwitting		upstart		useful	
unwonted		up-to-date		usefulness	
unworldly		uptown		useless	
unworthy		upward		usher	
unwrap		upholster		usual	
unwreathe		upholsterer		unusual	
unwritten		upholstery		usually	
unyielding		uranium		usury	
up		urban		usufruct	
upbraid		interurban		usurer	
upheaval		suburban		usurious	
upheld		urbane		usurp	
uphill		urbanity		usurpation	
uphold		urge		usurper	
upkeep		urged		utensil	
upland		urgency		utilize	
uplift		urgent		unutilized	
upmost		urn		utilitarian	
upon		use		utilitarianism	
upper		abuse		utility	

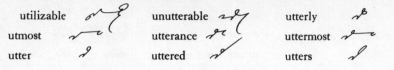

utilizable		unutterable		utterly	
utmost		utterance		uttermost	
utter		uttered		utters	

V

vacate
vacancy
vacant
vacation
vacationist
vaccinate
vaccination
vacillate
vacillation
vacuum
vacuity
vacuous
vagabond
vagary
vagrant
vagrancy
vague
vain
vainglory
vainness
vanity
valance
valedictory
valedictorian

valence
valentine
valerian
valet
valiant
valid
invalid
validate
validation
validity
validly
valise
valley
valor
valorous
value
evaluate
invaluable
revaluation
valuable
valuation
valueless
valve
valvular
vampire

vanadium
vanguard
vanilla
vanish
vanity
vanquish
vantage
vapid
vapor
evaporate
vaporization
vaporize
vaporous
varnish
vary
invariable
variability
variable
variance
variant
variation
variegate
variety
various
vassal

vassalage	vendible	verbal
vast	veneer	verbally
vaudeville	venerate	verbatim
vault	venerable	verbiage
vaulted	veneration	verbose
vaunt	vengeance	verbosity
vaunted	vengeful	verbena
vedette	venial	verdict
vegetable	venison	verdigris
vegetarian	venom	verdure
vegetarianism	venomous	verdant
vegetate	ventilate	verge
vegetation	unventilated	verify
vegetative	ventilation	verification
vehement	ventilator	verily
vehemence	ventricle	verisimilitude
vehicle	ventriloquism	veritable
vehicular	venture	veracious
velocipede	venturesome	verity
velocity	venturous	vermilion
velvet	venue	vermin
venal	veracity	vermicide
venality	veracious	vermiform
vend	veranda	vermifuge
vender	verb	verminous

vermuth
vernacular
vernal
vernier
versatility
versatile
verse
versification
versify
version
verso
versus
vertebra
vertebrae
vertebrate
vertex
vertical
vertigo
very
veriest
vesicle
vesper
vessel
vest
vestibule

vestige
vestigial
vestment
vestry
Vesuvian
veteran
veterinary
veto
vex
vexation
vexatious
viaduct
vial
viand
vibrate
vibrancy
vibrant
vibration
vibrational
vibrator
vibratory
vicar
vicarage
vicarious
viceroy

viceregal
vicinity
vicious
vicissitudes
victim
victimize
victor
victorious
victory
victual
viewed
interview
purview
review
vigil
vigilance
vigilant
vigor
vigorous
vile
vilification
vilify
village
villager
villain

villainous	virago	invisible
villainy	virgin	visibility
vindicate	virginal	visible
vindicable	virginity	visionary
vindication	virility	visual
vindicatory	virile	visualization
vindictive	virtue	visualize
vinegar	virtual	visually
vinaigrette	virtually	visit
vineyard	virtuous	revisited
vintage	virtuoso	visitation
viol	virtuosity	visitor
violate	virus	visor
inviolable	virulence	vista
violation	virulent	vital
violative	visa	devitalize
violator	visage	vitality
violence	viscera	vitalization
violent	viscid	vitalize
violet	viscidity	vitally
ultra-violet	viscosity	vitamin
violin	viscous	vitiate
violinist	viscount	vitiated
violoncello	vise	vitiation
viper	vision	vitrify

vitreous	vocally	voltmeter
vitrification	vocation	volubility
vitriol	non-vocational	voluble
vitriolic	vocational	volume
vituperate	vocationally	volumetric
vituperation	vociferous	voluminous
vituperative	voice	volunteer
vivacity	voiced	involuntary
vivacious	voiceless	voluntarily
vivid	void	voluntary
vivify	devoid	voluptuary
revivify	voidable	voluptuous
vivification	voided	volute
vivisect	volatility	vomit
vivisection	volatile	voracity
vivisectionist	volatilization	voracious
vivisector	volatilize	vortex
vixen	volcano	vote
vizier	volcanic	voted
vocabulary	volition	voter
vocal	volitional	votive
vocalism	volt	vouch
vocalist	voltage	vouched
vocalization	voltaic	voucher
vocalize	voltammeter	vouchsafe

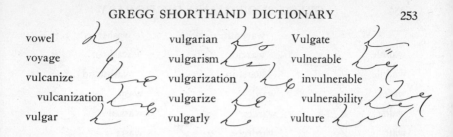

vowel	vulgarian	Vulgate
voyage	vulgarism	vulnerable
vulcanize	vulgarization	invulnerable
vulcanization	vulgarize	vulnerability
vulgar	vulgarly	vulture

W

wabble	warpath	washer
waddle	warrior	washout
wafer	warship	washstand
waffle	ward	wasp
waft	warden	wassail
wage	wardrobe	waste
wager	warehouse	wastage
Wagnerian	warm	wastebasket
wagon	warmed	wasteful
waist	warmth	wastrel
wait	warn	watch
wakeful	warned	watchcase
walk	warp	watchdog
walker	warrant	watchful
walkout	unwarrantable	watchmaker
walnut	warranted	watchman
walrus	warrantor	watch tower
waltz	warranty	watchword
wampum	warren	water
wander	wary	watercourse
want	unwary	waterfall
unwanted	was	waterfowl
war	wash	water-logged
warfare	unwashed	watermark
warlike	washable	watermelon

watershed	wealth	well-favored
water-tight	wealthily	welter
waterway	weapon	were
waterworks	weary	west
watery	wearily	westerly
watt	wearisome	western
wattage	weasel	westerner
wattmeter	weather	westward
waver	weather-beaten	wet
unwavering	weathercock	wetness
wax	weatherproof	whack
waxed	web	whale
waxen	week	whaleback
waxiness	weekday	whalebone
way	week-end	wharf
waybill	weekly	wharfage
wayfarer	weep	wharfinger
wayside	weight	wharves
wayward	weird	what
weak	welcome	somewhat
weaken	unwelcome	whatever
weakened	well	whatnot
weakling	unwell	whatsoever
weakly	welfare	wheat
weakness	well-born	wheaten

wheatworm	while	whither
wheel	whilom	whittle
when	whilst	who
whenever	whim	whoever
whensoever	whimsical	whole
whence	whimsicality	unwholesome
where	whine	whole-hearted
whereabouts	whip	wholesale
whereas	whipcord	wholesaler
whereat	whippet	wholesome
whereby	whipstock	wholly
wherefore	whirl	whoop
wherefrom	whirlpool	whose
wherein	whirlwind	why
whereof	whisk	wicked
whereon	whisky	wickedness
wheresoever	whisper	wickerwork
whereupon	whist	wicket
wherever	whistle	wide
wherewith	white	widen
wherewithal	whitecap	wideness
whether	whitefish	widespread
which	whiten	width
whichever	whiteness	widow
whichsoever	whitewood	widowed

widower	wine	witticism
widowhood	wineglass	wittily
wield	wing	wittiness
unwieldy	wingless	witch
wife	wink	witchery
wigwag	winner	with
wigwam	winter	notwithstanding
wild	wipe	within
wilderness	wiper	without
wildfire	wire	withdraw
wildness	wireless	withdrawal
will	wirepulling	withdrawn
unwilling	wise	withdrew
willful	unwise	withhold
willow	wisdom	withheld
wily	wisely	withstand
winch	wiser	withstood
wind	wisest	witness
wind	wish	wizard
windage	unwished	wizardry
windbreak	wisher	woe
windfall	wishful	woebegone
windily	wistaria	woeful
windmill	wit	wolf
window	unwitting	wolfhound

wolfish	wood	worker
wolverine	woodcraft	workhouse
wolves	woodcut	workman
woman	wooded	workmanship
unwomanly	wooden	workshop
womanhood	woodland	worktable
womankind	woodman	world
womanlike	woodpecker	unworldly
womanliness	woodsman	worldliness
womanly	woodwork	worldly
women	woodworm	worm
won	woof	hookworm
wonder	wool	worm-eaten
wonderful	woolen	wormhole
wonderland	word	wormwood
wonderment	worded	worry
wonderstricken	wordily	worried
wonderwork	wordiness	worriment
wondrous	wore	worrisome
won't	work	worse
wont	rework	worst
unwonted	unworkable	worship
woo	workable	worshiper
wooed	workaday	worshipful
wooer	worked	worshipped

worsted	wreath	wring
worth	wreck	wringer
unworthy	shipwreck	wrinkle
worthily	wreckage	wrist
worthiness	wrecker	writ
worthless	wrench	write
worthy	wrest	rewrite
would	wrestle	writer
wound	wrestler	written
wounded	wretch	wrong
wound	wretchedness	wronged
wove	wriggle	wrongful
wraith	wright	wrong-headed
wrangle	millwright	wrongly
wrath	playwright	wrongness
wrathful	shipwright	wroth

X, Y, Z

xebec	yell	yule
xenon	yellow	yuletide
xylophone	yeoman	zeal
yacht	yeomanry	zealot
yachtsman	yes	zealotry
yak	yesterday	zealous
yam	yet	zebra
yank	yield	zebu
yard	unyielding	zenith
yardage	yodel	zephyr
yardarm	yolk	Zeppelin
yardstick	you-your	zero
yarn	yourself	zest
yawl	young	zigzag
ye	younger	zinc
yea	youngest	Zion
year	youngish	zircon
yearbook	youngster	zirconium
yearling	youth	zither
yearly	youthful	zodiac
yearn	youthfulness	zone
yeast	ytterbium	zoölogy
	yttrium	zwieback